For God and Country

The Pietà of Joan of Arc
(sculpture in bronze by Daniel A. E. Balan)

Fr. Michael Joseph Cerrone III

For God and Country

The Heroic Life and Martyrdom of St. Joan of Arc

SOPHIA INSTITUTE PRESS
Manchester, New Hampshire

Copyright © 2015 by Michael Joseph Cerrone III

Maps Copyright © 2015 by John Folley

Illustrations Copyright © 2015 by Mary Lawrence N. Kennickell

Cover design by Coronation Media in collaboration with Perceptions Design Studio.

On the cover: *The Entrance of Joan of Arc (1412–31) into Orleans on 8th May 1429* (oil on canvas), Jean-Jacques Scherrer (1855–1916) / Musee des Beaux-Arts, Orleans, France / Bridgeman Images.

Printed in the United States of America. All rights reserved.

Biblical references in this book are taken from the Catholic Edition of the Revised Standard Version of the Bible, copyright 1965, 1966 by the Division of Christian Education of the National Council of the Churches of Christ in the United States of America. Used by permission. All rights reserved.

No part of this book may be reproduced, stored in a retrieval system, or transmitted in any form, or by any means, electronic, mechanical, photocopying, or otherwise, without the prior written permission of the publisher, except by a reviewer, who may quote brief passages in a review.

Sophia Institute Press
Box 5284, Manchester, NH 03108
1-800-888-9344

www.SophiaInstitute.com

Sophia Institute Press® is a registered trademark of Sophia Institute.

Library of Congress Cataloging-in-Publication Data
Cerrone, Michael Joseph.
  For God and country : the heroic life and martyrdom of St. Joan of Arc / Fr. Michael Joseph Cerrone III.
      pages cm
  Includes bibliographical references.
  ISBN 978-1-62282-242-3 (pbk. : alk. paper) 1. Joan, of Arc, Saint, 1412-1431. 2. Christian women saints—France—Biography. 3. Meditations. I. Title.
  DC103.C475 2015
  944'.026092—dc23
  [B]
                                                                            2014039786

In memory of my parents,
Michael Joseph Cerrone Jr.,
Army combat infantryman in WWII and Vietnam
and teacher of American history and civics,
and Menna Dorothy Cerrone,
loyal American citizen and devoted wife and mother,
who taught and lived the love
for God and country;
and in honor of those military men and women
who strive to live virtuously
in selfless service to their nation
for the cause of freedom, justice, and peace.

Contents

Preface ix

Introduction: The Church, Europe,
and France in the Middle Ages 3

I. The Wise Maiden 15

II. The Religious Patriot 31

III. The Holy Warrior 47

IV. The Invincible Prisoner 109

V. The Heroic Martyr 135

VI. The Nation Reborn 153

VII. The Church Renewed 171

    Conclusion 199

    Prayers 207

    Bibliography 215

Stained-glass window of Saint Michael the Archangel and Saint Joan of Arc in the Chapel of the Most Holy Trinity, West Point, New York.

Preface

In the Chapel of the Most Holy Trinity at West Point, New York, the stained-glass windows along the side walls depict various patron saints of soldiers, among them Michael the Archangel, prince of the heavenly army of angels; George (Asia Minor) and Maurice (Africa), soldiers and martyrs of the early Christian era; the veteran soldiers Martin of Tours (France) and Ignatius of Loyola (Spain); and very prominently next to the archangel, Joan of Arc, the Maid of Lorraine (France) and soldier-martyr for God and country.

    I first noticed that particular window of the lone female soldier-saint during my freshman year of college as a seventeen-year-old cadet at the United States military academy. It did not occur to me then that Joan was the same age when, after being called by God, she was appointed by her future king to be the soldier-leader of a small army loyal to France and rallied a demoralized people to initiate the liberation of their homeland. Nor did I know in 1964 that the Catholic Church had declared her to be a saint of God only in 1920, nearly five hundred years after her death at nineteen years of age by burning at the stake in Rouen, France, on May 30, 1431.

Many more years of my life passed before I realized the full significance of her extraordinary, heroic witness, not only for the nation of France but also for other nations whose citizens profess a love for the one true God and for their home countries. After more than five years of U.S. Army service as an infantry and military intelligence officer in the Vietnam War and the Cold War, a year of music and international relations studies, and then six years of seminary and parish work, I was ordained a priest in 1981.

Returning in 1990 to army service in the chaplain corps, whose motto is *Pro Deo et patria* ("for God and country"), I served in the Persian Gulf War of 1991 and later in other troop assignments. But it was not until a few months after the terrorist attacks of September 11, 2001, that I finally learned from a fellow Catholic chaplain that my priestly ordination day and Saint Joan of Arc's feast day are the same—the same day also as the traditional Memorial Day, on which we honor all war dead of the United States of America. Joan's spirit of religious devotion and patriotic duty began to exert a strong influence on me.

In the Lord God's great plan, historical coincidences are really providential times of grace for us. My priesthood, which began exactly 550 years from the day of Joan's death, is now a constant reminder for me to imitate Jeanne *La Pucelle* (Joan the Maiden) by leading souls in religious fidelity to God and compassionate charity to others. Twenty years of active military service, the last fifteen as a chaplain, made me appreciate more fully the virtue of patriotism, the love of one's country, which Joan embodied by selfless service to her king and her people, at the cost of her own life.

Memorial Day too has its special poignancy for me in honoring "the last full measure of devotion" rendered by my friends and classmates killed in Vietnam during the war against atheistic

PREFACE

communism, and by many others who sacrificed themselves in past battles against all enemies, both foreign and domestic. Those quoted words of Abraham Lincoln, first addressed as a tribute to the thousands of fallen soldiers after the bloody battle at Gettysburg during the American Civil War, apply equally to all who have died fighting their nations' wars against tyranny and oppression. Memorial Day remembrances now also honor the last full measure of devotion by those killed in the present-day global war on terrorism.

These complementary virtues of religion and patriotism are increasingly evident in many of today's military men and women, who serve as guardians of peace, defenders of life, and enforcers of justice, at home and abroad. With Joan of Arc, they extend the divine legacy of noble, godly souls who demonstrate single-minded devotion to a just or holy cause. Yet not only military personnel but all citizens need these virtues, particularly during times of cultural clashes and religious wars, raging even in this new millennium of Christianity. Every person of every nation in every epoch of world history can imitate the timeless model of heroic virtue that Joan of Arc reveals — a beautiful reflection of Jesus Christ.

In the last two years of her life, as a combat soldier and a prisoner of war, Joan the Maiden encountered opposition to her mission; a demoralized army; divided loyalties among the clergy, nobility, and commoners in the towns and districts of her occupied homeland; and during her trial, the treachery of churchmen in league with the enemy. Nevertheless, she remained faithful and true to Almighty God in the Church's sacramental life and to the heavenly Voices in her own prayer life. She vigorously protected her virginity and promoted piety and good morals, especially chastity, among her troops. And she was courageous, disciplined, and bold in leading battlefield operations, despite injury to herself and danger of death.

Perhaps most unusual for a leader in warfare, La Pucelle personally and compassionately tended many combat casualties, not only her own French soldiers but English troops as well. She wept over the loss of human life, so grieved was she in the depths of her pure heart and gentle soul. She was especially concerned over any soldier who died in battle without a prior good confession of his sins. And in her final and most Christlike act of mercy before being burned to death, she forgave her enemies and even asked forgiveness of anyone she may have offended in her lifetime.

Catholic Faith and fundamental moral principles always guided Joan of Arc in her quest for justice and peace in the social order. She clearly understood the divine purpose of her human life; and with indefatigable resolve she accomplished her mission on behalf of her country. With God's amazing grace in her soul, and even after her death, she inspired the king and people of France to fulfill their own mission of restoring themselves as one nation under God.

This literary offering is not an attempt at scholarship about Joan's life. Rather it is my humble meditation on her legacy of virtue, always victorious over vice. Saint Joan of Arc, in her heroic and enduring love for God and country, continues to inspire those who come to know her. Almighty God continues to grace and bless those who follow her noble example of virtue, as she followed Christ in doing the Father's will. May God help us fulfill our own social, religious, and civic duties. Let us work together for reconciliation with God and neighbor, unity within Christ's Church, justice and respect for every human being, and peace among all nations on earth.

—Father Michael Joseph Cerrone III
Catholic priest and retired U.S. Army chaplain

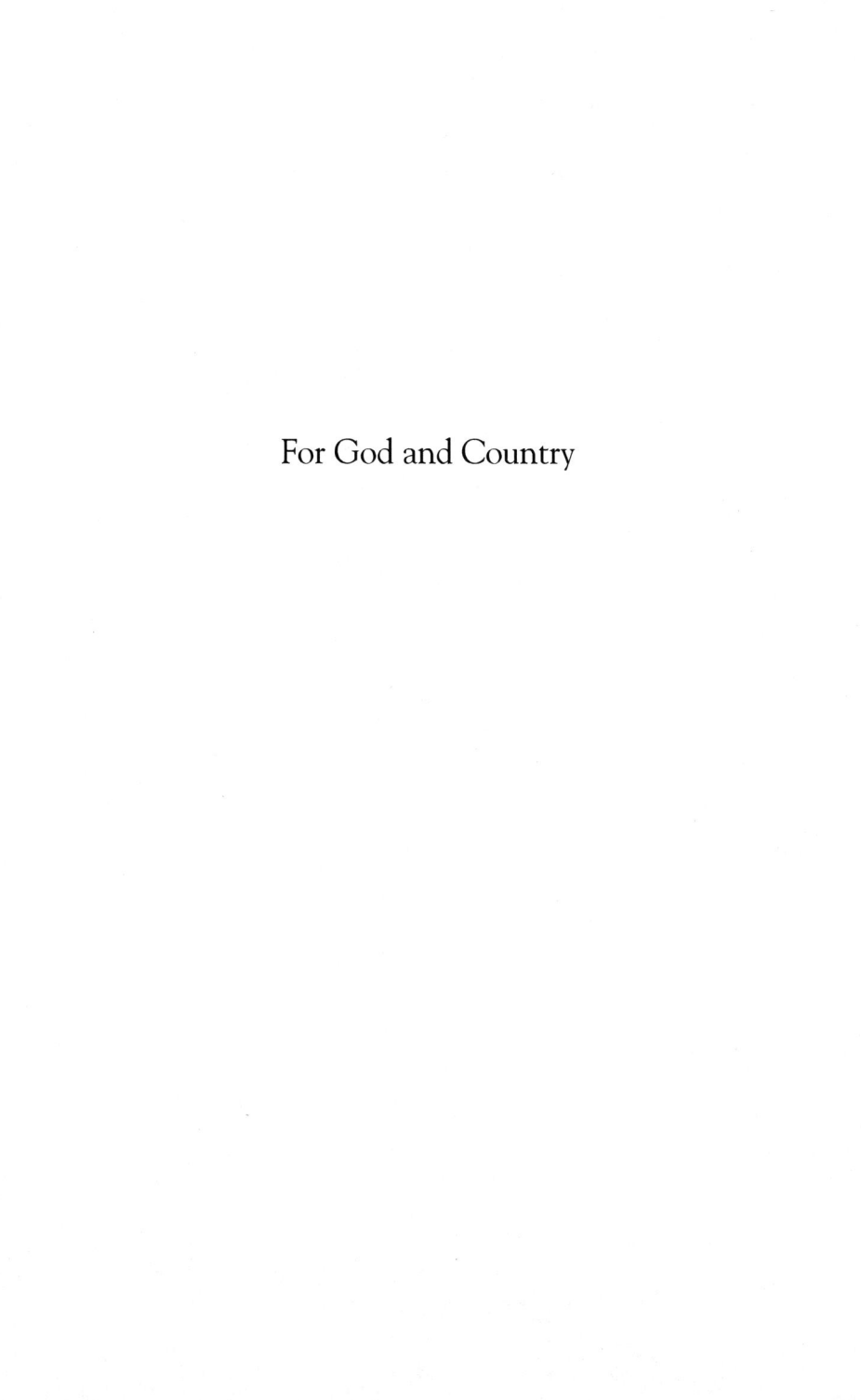

For God and Country

Introduction

The Church, Europe, and France in the Middle Ages

War was the main threat to people during late medieval times throughout the countryside of what is modern-day France. In fact, historians call that period from the early fourteenth to the mid-fifteenth century the Hundred Years' War, during which expansionist England battled with politically fractured France in an internecine contest for the territory and the soul of a nation.

Intermarriage among the royal families of medieval Europe was the customary way to build alliances and promote security and peace among nations. But with family feuds over land and resources, prestige and power, those marital arrangements could result as easily in theft, murder, and mayhem as in any mutual benefits to the peoples of those countries. Moreover, the common folk of those nationalities and provinces, especially the unprotected civilian populations, always suffered most severely. Human nature in aristocrats could manifest as many vices as virtues, despite the cultural assimilation of a thousand years of official Catholic Christianity. The nobility were too often quite ignoble in their attitudes and actions. Pride, envy, anger, avarice, lust, gluttony, and sloth in a king and his local lords tended to foster a social climate of irreligion and immorality among commoners in the cities and towns of those realms.

The practice of Christianity had become legalized throughout Europe soon after the Roman emperor Constantine halted the persecutions of Christians by his pagan predecessors. Yet paganism and barbarism, along with heretical sectarianism, persisted and periodically reversed the growth of the Christian Church among the European peoples. In the region of the Gauls, the baptism of Clovis, king of the Franks, in A.D. 496 marked a major advance for the Church in that realm. In 732 Charles Martel won the Battle of Tours against an invading Moorish force from Africa, saving Christendom from militant Islam. In 751 Pepin III became king of the Franks with the blessing of the last Greek pope, Saint Zacharias. Three years later, Pepin marched with his army into Italy to save the papacy from invading barbarian Lombards. His son Charles succeeded him as sole king of the Franks in 771.[1]

Known to history as Charlemagne, Charles the Great zealously promoted an extraordinary rebirth of Christian faith and culture during his forty-five-year reign into the early ninth century. He fostered learning in academics, art, and architecture in cathedral schools and monasteries for clergy and religious communities and for laymen under his patronage. Those centers of education eventually became known as universities. Although crowned as Holy Roman emperor by Pope Leo III in the year 800, Charlemagne himself placed the crown on his son's head as his successor in order to maintain royal independence from papal interference.

---

[1] Matthew Bunson, *Encyclopedia of Catholic History* (Huntington, IN: Our Sunday Visitor, 2004), 326–327.

After Charlemagne's death, the empire divided into three parts. By the end of the ninth century, France had become a distinct political state under a monarch from among the feudal lords.[2]

In the region of the Angles, Saxons, and Jutes, Christianity spread also to Brittania, as the Romans called it. By the end of the sixth century, thanks largely to the evangelization efforts of Bishop Saint Augustine of Canterbury, sent there by Pope Saint Gregory the Great, the Church became well established throughout the island. In the seventh century and into the eighth, Benedictine monks promoted learning and the arts, bringing Anglo-Saxon culture to a high level of refinement and producing saints among the clergy and even the royalty. Despite an invasion by barbarous Danes in the eighth century, King Alfred the Great fostered a temporary rebirth of Christian culture in England. More lasting reforms continued under the influence of Archbishop Saint Dunston of Canterbury. King Saint Edward the Confessor, the last Saxon ruler of England, introduced Norman influences from the Continent into English culture before his death in 1066, the same year that William I, Duke of Normandy, invaded the island, with enormous historical consequences for both England and France.[3]

William the Conqueror defeated his rival in England at the battle of Hastings and then firmly established his reign throughout England by his military might, while closely collaborating with the pope in the spiritual pacification of the clans and fiefdoms. At his death in 1087, princes, dukes, earls, and other feudal lords vied with one another for domination of their own lands or of the entire island.

[2] Ibid., 327
[3] Ibid., 289–290.

Fifty years later, in 1137, an ambitious, powerful, and sophisticated female aristocrat, Eleanor of Aquitaine, became queen of France. She reigned with her husband, King Louis VII, until 1152, when their marriage was dissolved by local Church officials for the dubious reason of failing to produce a male heir to the throne of France. Two years later Eleanor became queen of England upon her marriage to Henry II, the king who in 1170 arranged the murder of his former friend, Archbishop Saint Thomas à Becket in his own Canterbury Cathedral. As England's queen, Eleanor remained in control of her vast land holdings in her home region of southwestern France until her death in 1189. Her heirs claimed title to those lands as their ancestral inheritance. The stage was being set in late twelfth-century England for the commencement in early fourteenth-century France of a hundred years of war between the two nations.

The entire Church had been suffering longer and from more serious internal wounds because of the sins of her own children, both clergy and laity, than even from foreign Islamic invasions into Christendom by Moors, Saracens, and Turks. Many clergy, including some bishops and even a few popes, practiced nepotism or lived immorally in violation of their oaths of celibate chastity. Furthermore, aristocratic prelates could be ruthless toward political opponents. Religious orders too, whose members vowed poverty, sometimes amassed great wealth by simony — that is, profiting from the sale of religious indulgences, Church offices, or the like — thus scandalizing many of their fellow Christians.

The first major schism in Christendom began in 1054 between Byzantine and Latin-rite Christians. Church politics between popes and patriarchs and national politics among emperors and kings created rifts within the Eastern and Western wings of the Church, and this obviously affected the peoples in the lands ruled by Christian monarchs. In addition, heresies against Christian doctrine arose like weeds in the Lord's vineyard, as during ancient Christian times.

Despite several attempts at reconciliation, the internal breach deepened after a number of other unfortunate events: the papal excommunication of the emperor in Constantinople; the Crusaders' pillaging of that Christian city instead of liberating it from the invading Islamic armies; and contentions over ecclesiastical jurisdictions and papal primacy. These incidents adversely affected the unity of the universal Church probably as much as did doctrinal disputations by Orthodox versus Catholic theologians about how the divine Persons proceed within the Godhead of the Most Holy Trinity.

Meanwhile, in twelfth-century France, several noteworthy theologians and writers, such as Peter Abelard and Saint Anselm, and the great mystic, monk, and preacher Saint Bernard of Clairvaux, emerged. Bernard exhorted the pope and Christian kings throughout Christendom to undertake a crusade against the Muslims to regain the sacred sites in the Holy Land. Yet, the greatest era in France's history, surpassing in tranquillity even the rule of Charlemagne, was in the thirteenth century under the glorious, forty-four-year reign of King Saint Louis IX. Louis was the model Christian king who epitomized the ideals of piety, chivalry, charity, and humility. He was also a model husband and father, always faithful in devotion to his wife and patient in the instruction of his children.

During King Louis's rule from 1226 to 1270, the Church in France boasted the University of Paris as the premier Catholic university in Christendom, producing such luminaries of theology and spirituality as Saints Albert the Great, Thomas Aquinas, and Bonaventure. Gothic art and architecture flourished under the saintly monarch's reign, such that the magnificent cathedral of Notre Dame de Paris and the breathtakingly beautiful Sainte Chapelle (Holy Chapel), and the cathedrals of Chartres, Amiens, and Reims dotted the landscapes of France. Church and state were interdependent, the head of each respecting the other's prerogatives and cooperating in unity for the common good. The French people enjoyed domestic tranquillity and economic prosperity mainly because of King Louis's true humility and sanctity in deference and devotion to the hierarchy of Christ's Church. Church and state relations were never more harmonious in service to the people.

When he received an urgent summons from the pope, King Louis himself led an army on the Seventh Crusade; but he was captured by the Muslims in 1250, was ransomed the next year, and returned to France to reform the government only after his mother's death in 1254. He forbade private warfare, distributed taxes more equitably, and extended legal rights of judicial appeal to the crown itself. Inopportunely, Saint Louis launched the Eighth Crusade, and after capturing Carthage, he fell ill from the plague and died in 1270. The Latin Church still remembers his holy death on August 25 as his feast day.[4]

King Louis's successors, however, were neither so saintly nor so humble. Church and state relations quickly deteriorated under the arrogant King Philip IV, crowned in 1285. Philip began to assert his state authority over papal authority in the Church, demanding taxes from the clergy and religious orders, despite the objections of the pope. He humiliated and physically harassed Pope Boniface VIII, hastening his death. Philip then "persuaded" the newly elected Frenchman, Pope Clement V, in 1309, to take

---

[4] Bunson, *Encyclopedia of Catholic History*, 517–518.

up residence in Avignon, France, rather than in Rome. Clement meekly agreed, acquiescing so completely to the tyrannical monarch that he published a papal bull endorsing the prerogatives of France's king and giving special preference to the kingdom of France: "Like the people of Israel ... the kingdom of France, as a special people chosen by the Lord to carry out the orders of Heaven, is distinguished by special marks of honor and grace."[5]

Several of his successor popes remained in Avignon, under intense political pressure from the French kings. Simultaneously, that century-long war between England and France began, along with the internal conflicts over French territories among the rival principalities and duchies in France. By mid-century, one of those French popes, despite his former monastic life of vowed poverty, turned his austere residence into a luxurious papal palace fit for a king. King Philip "the Fair" had initiated what historians call the Avignon Papacy, a seventy-year period in which the kings of France controlled the election of Catholic popes.

Heeding the exhortations of two holy mystics, the elderly Saint Bridget of Sweden and the young Saint Catherine of Siena, Italy, the French pope Blessed Urban V returned to the Vatican in 1367, to the great delight of the Romans. In an attempt to heal the Eastern Schism, the Byzantine emperor Henry IV then traveled to Rome to pledge his belief in the primacy of the Roman pontiff and in the Catholic *Filioque* doctrine (that the Holy Spirit proceeds from the Father *and the Son*). Sadly, Emperor Henry could not bring the Orthodox clergymen into the agreement, since they stubbornly held the erroneous view that the Holy Spirit proceeds from God the Father alone. Pope Urban,

---

[5] Deborah A. Fraioli, *Joan of Arc and the Hundred Years War* (Westport, CT: Greenwood Press, 2005), 53.

upon hearing about a new outbreak of war between England and France and disaffected also by the fickleness and infighting of the Italian aristocrats and their clergy, decided to return to Avignon, despite Saint Bridget's prophetic warning of his death there if he did so. He ignored her, and within three months of his return to his familiar surroundings, he died, in December 1370.

The eleven cardinals who assembled in Avignon unanimously elected Gregory XI in just two days. Gregory wanted to return immediately with his cardinals to Rome but unfortunately was prevented for seven years from making the journey because of continuing armed conflicts among the Italian city states, including the Papal States. Nevertheless, Gregory vigorously disciplined the mendicant religious orders and fought heresies through the Inquisition, filling the jails of France with those who had avoided a death sentence. Elsewhere too the Church hierarchy had to contend with heretics and their adherents who challenged various teachings of Christ. Western ecclesiastical courts of inquisition usually dealt a death sentence to those who refused to recant their errors and who fomented rebellion from Church and state authorities, all of whom were Catholic then. The pope also dreamed of a new Crusade to relieve Constantinople and restore unity with the Greek Byzantine branch of the Church. Aware of the prophetic insistence of those two saintly mystics, Pope Gregory returned for the last year of his pontificate to the Holy See of Saint Peter as Bishop of Rome and Vicar of Christ.

The Avignon Papacy began as a political accommodation by a Roman pontiff submitting to a French monarch; but it eventually developed into a major religious crisis within the Latin branch of the Church. Other political factions in Europe, obviously resentful of French control of the papacy, supported aristocratic cardinals from their own nations or regions as candidates for pope. By 1380, the year of Catherine of Siena's death, two men claimed the papacy, a pope and an antipope. The Romans rioted during the next conclave and demanded that an Italian be their pope. The fearful cardinals yielded and elected an irascible Italian, Urban VI, who succeeded only in alienating most of the Church hierarchy and the kings of Europe by his abusive and bellicose ways. The authenticity of his election by the cardinals under duress was contested by the kingdoms of France, Scotland, and Naples, who supported another man in Avignon. The hated Italian pope died in 1389, presumably of poisoning. By 1412, the year of Joan of Arc's birth, the international politics of papal succession had produced three claimants as pope, only one of whom could be the true successor to the Prince of the Apostles.

These popes and antipopes and their supporting monarchs created the political and religious chaos known as the Great Western Schism, which lasted nearly forty years, into the early fifteenth century. The kingdom of Christ's Church on earth, like the kingdom of France, was indeed in a very pitiful state. The mixture of politics and religion, churchmen and statesmen meddling in the others' business, had again grievously wounded the Church, already suffering from the rift with Byzantine Christianity. In 1415 Pope Gregory XII reconvened the Council of Constance under his own authority as true pope, and then abdicated the papacy, as he had promised, in order to end the terrible schism.

For two years, a reunited college of cardinals at the Council of Constance discussed papal electoral procedures. Then in 1417 they unanimously elected the next pope, Martin V. He soon sent peace missions to England and France, while continuing negotiations in Constantinople for a reunion between Greek and Roman churches. But papal attempts to reconcile those two warring nations and the two major branches of Christianity were unsuccessful. To add misery to the mayhem, periodic outbreaks of the dreaded bubonic plague decimated populations in various parts of Europe. All the while, Islamic military forces of Saracens, followed by Ottoman Turks from Asia Minor, continued to threaten eastern Christendom and the Balkan Peninsula, as, earlier in the Middle Ages, the Moors had penetrated far into the Iberian Peninsula, with Mohammed's religion of "conversion by coercion."

Back in England, rival feudal lords fought each other for the rights of royal succession and possession of the English crown. Their kings also periodically sent military forces into France to reinforce their claims to ancestral lands. In the ascendancy was Henry V of England, an intrepid warrior who became king. At the same time, the loose confederation of French principalities had begun splintering apart because of the divided loyalties and rivalries among their own princes and dukes from the various provinces. The armed conflicts between English and French aristocrats and their opposing armies became also a civil war between rival Armagnacs and Burgundians and others fighting within France for control of that crown and kingdom.

After seventy-five years of war, the kingdom of France was in a truly pathetic state. The French had suffered a humiliating defeat at Agincourt in 1415 by a much smaller English army commanded by their king, Henry V. France's King Charles VI, suffering from psychosis and dementia with only brief periods of lucidity, agreed to the Treaty of Troyes in 1420. His queen, Isabeau of Bavaria, collaborated in that treaty, giving their daughter in marriage to the ambitious King Henry V of England, so that a son of theirs would become king of both England and France at the death of Charles VI. The same treaty thus disinherited Charles and Isabeau's only surviving adult son, the dauphin (crown prince) Charles VII, from rightfully assuming his father's throne.

Furthermore, the murder of the Duke of Orléans by his rival, the Duke of Burgundy, precipitated the revenge murder of the Duke of Burgundy by allies of Charles VII. Charles's mother, Isabeau, a promiscuous woman and obese in her later years, agreed with Duke Philip of Burgundy about her son's complicity in the revenge murder of Philip's father. She also probably insinuated that Charles himself was the result of her illicit affair with her husband's cousin, the murdered Duke of Orléans. Thus, on account of both his alleged involvement in murder and his presumably illegitimate birth, the signatories of the Treaty of Troyes opposed Charles as not entitled to succeed his father as king of France. A blood feud between two cousins became the accelerant fuel for the flames of war between two nations. Although Original Sin comes "in the blood" at human conception and is absolved by God in Christian baptism, concupiscence, the weakness of the flesh to temptation, remains part of the human condition. We might call this a disloyalty of royalty, which demonstrates that the "blood royal" of France, and of Germanic Bavaria, had as much actual sin in it as the blood of an Englishman.

Adding to the confusion and fear among the people were the ambitions, intrigues, and divided loyalties among many churchmen within opposing camps, which also clouded the religious climate in late medieval Europe. Nevertheless, despite the turmoil of the Hundred Years' War in that dark age of France, Almighty God revealed a radiant and luminous personality—"a sign that would be opposed" (cf. Luke 2:34). From a tiny, obscure frontier village bordering the lands of France and Germany, another saintly young woman mystic came forth to lead the way of true devotion to God and country.

I

The Wise Maiden

Wisdom has built her house,
she has set up her seven pillars.
She has sent out her maids to call
from the highest places in the town,
"Whoever is simple, let him turn in here!"

—Proverbs 9:1, 3–4

And Jesus increased in wisdom and in stature,
and in favor with God and man.

—Luke 2:52

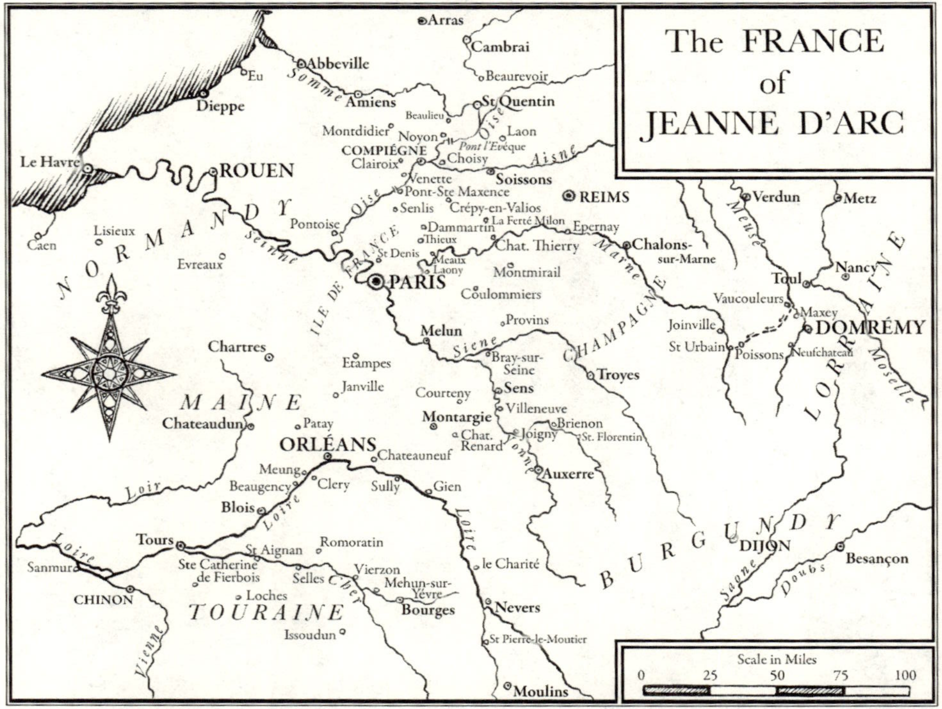
The FRANCE
of
JEANNE D'ARC
NORMANDY
ILE DE FRANCE
CHAMPAGNE
LORRAINE
MAINE
TOURAINE
BURGUNDY
Arras
Cambrai
Abbeville
Eu
Beaurevoir
Somme
Dieppe
Amiens
St Quentin
Beaulieu
Montdidier
Noyon
Laon
Oise
Pont l'Evêque
COMPIÉGNE
Clairoix
Choisy
Aisne
Le Havre
ROUEN
Venette
Soissons
Pont-Ste Maxence
REIMS
Senlis
Crépy-en-Valios
La Ferté Milon
Dammartin
Epernay
Thieux
Chat. Thierry
Chalons-sur-Marne
Pontoise
Lisieux
Caen
Seinne
St Denis
Meaux
Laony
Marne
Evreaux
Montmirail
PARIS
Coulommiers
Provins
Melun
Siene
Chartres
Etampes
Bray-sur-Seine
Troyes
Janville
Courteny
Sens
Villeneuve
Montargie
Chateaudun
Patay
Brienon
Chat. Renard
Joigny
St. Florentin
ORLÉANS
Chateauneuf
Yonne
Auxerre
Meung
Clery
Sully
Gien
Beaugency
Loir
Blois
Loire
Tours
St Aignan
Romoratin
Sanmur
Ste Catherine de Fierbois
Vierzon
le Charité
Selles
Cher
Mehun-sur-Yèvre
CHINON
Loches
Bourges
Nevers
Issoudun
Vienne
St Pierre-le-Moutier
Moulins
Verdun
Metz
Meuse
Nancy
Toul
Vaucouleurs
Maxey
Joinville
DOMRÉMY
St Urbain
Poissons
Neufchateau
Moselle
DIJON
Besançon
Saone
Doubs
Scale in Miles
0
25
50
75
100

⚜

Light from Above

On the east-central frontier of that divided kingdom of early fifteenth-century France, in the southern outskirts of the wartorn province of Lorraine was the very small, unfortified village of Domrémy. That village was named after the apostolic bishop to the Gauls, Saint Remigius (Remi in French), who had baptized Clovis in Reims and anointed him with a mysterious, heaven-sent holy oil as the first Christian king of the Franks. Most villagers in Domrémy were good Christians, faithful to God and to the Church, and loyal to the king of France. They were generally modest and peaceable in their rural community life.

But the townsfolk were constantly vulnerable to marauding bands of armed renegades or to advancing Burgundian troops allied with England. Even the Germanic Duke of Saarbruck to the east once burned Domrémy to the ground because its citizens failed to pay him the taxes he demanded. To avoid the rape, pillage, and plunder by brigands and derelict soldiers, the villagers frequently retreated to the nearby castle towns of Vaucouleurs and Neufchâteau, whose citizens were also loyal to the French monarchy. Long periods of peace and security were rare during the many years of war.

Next to the village church of Domrémy was the small, humble house of Jacques Darc (d'Arc) and his wife, Isabelle Romée. They were a simple, pious, hard-working, and highly respected couple, who were active in their church and in leadership of their community, while also managing their portion of the farmland and tending to domestic chores. Jacques was a village leader who represented his community in economic and civic matters in Vaucouleurs and in Neufchâteau. Isabelle Romée was accomplished in sewing, spinning, and weaving cloth and often went on pilgrimages to holy shrines. She probably received the name Romée because of a prior pilgrimage to the city of Rome, center of Christendom, where Saint Peter had been martyred in the year 67.

On January 6, 1412, the great feast day of the Epiphany of the Lord, their fifth child was born, a daughter whom they named Jehanne (the medieval French spelling of Jeanne). Legend has it that marvelous heavenly lights, which brought wonder and joy to Domrémy that night, foretold the arrival of a special child; much as the mysterious Star of David had lighted the way of the three wise men to the Christ Child in the little town of Bethlehem.

Vocation and Mission

Jeanne (Joan), or Jeannette, as family and fellow villagers affectionately called her, was an obedient child, cheerful and ready to assist her mother at home and occasionally her father in the fields. Isabelle taught her young daughter Jeannette to pray the Pater Noster (the Our Father), the Ave Maria (the Hail Mary), and the Credo (the Apostles' Creed, or profession of faith), along with other devotional practices of good Catholics. As she grew in age, wisdom, and grace, Jeannette frequently attended Holy Mass, even on weekdays, confessed her sins often, and visited nearby shrines honoring the Blessed Virgin Mary and patron saints. "I learned my faith and was correctly taught to do as a good child should.... From my mother I learned the 'Paternoster,' the 'Ave,' and the Creed; I had my teaching in the faith from her and from no one else."[6]

From her early childhood, Jeannette was remembered for her love of God and His saints. Whenever she heard the village church bells ringing, she paused from her chores or her play, looked toward the church, and recited the Angelus prayer, recalling the Archangel Gabriel's announcement to the Virgin Mary God willed for her to become the Mother of His divine Son. Often she left her friends and went to the small church to attend Mass. Jeannette's parish priest testified to her beautiful Christian character, deep piety, and profound respect for the Church, including the clergy, the holy places, her elders, and her fellow Christians. Without affectation or self-consciousness, Jeannette lived as easily in the supernatural realm of the divine by prayer as in the natural course of events in ordinary human relationships and activities.

Jeannette was congenial and vibrant also outside the home in the neighborhood and had both male and female friends. Occasionally the girls would visit a lovely tree in the area, which some called the Fairy Tree and others the Lady Tree, perhaps wishing each would grow up to find a good man to marry. But Jeannette would only gather beautiful flowers from there to bring to the shrine of the Madonna of Bermont, two kilometers

---

[6] Andrea Hopkins, *Six Medieval Women* (New York: Barnes and Noble, 1997); quote from the trial transcript.

away from Domrémy. "Jeanne went willingly to church and frequented holy places: I know—for when I was young I went several times with her on pilgrimage to the hermitage of Notre Dame de Bermont; she went to that hermitage every Saturday [Our Lady's Day] with her sister, and she lighted candles."[7] This was Michel Lebuin's main recollection of his childhood experiences with Jeannette.

The boys and occasionally some of the girls too would duel with long sticks, pretending to be soldiers of rivaling regions of France. If they lived in the nearby village of Maxey, which sided with the Duke of Burgundy in an alliance with the English monarchy, the children there pretended to be Burgundian soldiers. But if they lived in Domrémy, the youngsters dueled as Armagnac soldiers, loyal to the French king and his heir apparent, the dauphin Charles Valois VII. Jeannette never pretended to fight on the side of the Burgundians, who she thought were betraying France and its Christian monarchy.

From her early years Jeannette's charitable nature and compassion became evident in her care for the sick and the elderly. She frequently visited even those who were not her relatives and prayed for and consoled them with genuine sympathy. Her very presence would lift hearts and spirits that were otherwise lonely or disconsolate. She generously gave alms to the poor from her own modest resources.

Like all the village girls and most of the boys, Jeannette was unschooled and could neither read nor write. But unlike many other children, she always listened very carefully to instructions

---

[7] George H. Tavard, *The Spiritual Way of St. Jeanne d'Arc* (Collegeville, MN: Liturgical Press, 1998), 75 quote from Jules Quicherat's edition.

from her elders and did her chores willingly and conscientiously. Whether spinning the wool, weaving, or sewing, she prided herself on the speed and precision with which she performed her tasks. Sometimes she took her turn tending the livestock of family and fellow villagers. Noteworthy also was her diligence in completing her daily duties for the love of God, her parents and family, and her village.

"I had a daughter born in holy wedlock; she grew up amid the fields and pastures. I had her baptized and confirmed and brought her up in the fear of God. I taught her respect for the traditions of the Church; and I succeeded so well that she spent much of her time in church, and after going to Confession, she received the Eucharist frequently. Because the people suffered so much, she had a great compassion for them in her heart; and despite her youth she would fast and pray for them with great devotion and fervor. She never thought, spoke or did anything against the faith." Thus did the elderly, frail Isabelle Romée later testify about her daughter Jehanne.[8]

Joan made a private vow of virginity at age thirteen after she heard her Voices. Saint Michael the Archangel, prince of the heavenly host of angels, was the first one she saw and heard. Then two late-third-century virgin martyrs, Saint Catherine of Alexandria (Egypt) and Saint Margaret of Antioch (Asia Minor), also appeared and spoke to Joan. All three heavenly visitors called her Jeanne La Pucelle (Joan the Virgin or Maiden) and *fille de Dieu* (daughter of God). "When I was thirteen, I had a Voice from God to help me govern myself." Joan then made a private vow of virginity "'for as long as it pleases God' ... because in the

---

[8] Donald Spoto, *Joan: The Mysterious Life of the Heretic Turned Saint* (New York: HarperSanFranciso, 2007), 187.

depths of her being she was transformed by the encounter [with the archangel]. She suddenly acquired a whole new purpose in life ... through an exclusive commitment to God. 'I must keep the vow and promise I have made to our Lord, to keep well my virginity of body and of soul.'"[9]

In 1428 Burgundians raided Domrémy and burned the parish church, forcing the sixteen-year-old Joan and her family to seek refuge in Neufchâteau. While there she was cited by a Church tribunal in Toul for refusing a marriage contract. Joan's father had previously arranged a marriage for her with a young man from a neighboring town because he feared for his daughter's moral integrity as a single young woman. He was greatly troubled by strange dreams that Joan would leave home with soldiers. He thus assumed she would lose her integrity and bring shame on the family name. He would rather she die than lose her soul; and he even instructed her older brothers to drown her if she tried to leave!

"My father and my mother watched me closely and kept me under severe subjection.... I obeyed them in everything except my departure.... Since it was God who commanded it, if I had a hundred fathers and a hundred mothers, or if I had been the daughter of a king, I would have left.... My father and my mother almost went out of their minds when I left for Vaucouleurs."[10] Since Joan herself had never consented to the marriage, the Toul tribunal dismissed the young man's claim and thus freed her to live by her privately professed vow of virginal chastity. Her resolute will to remain a virgin "as long as it pleases God"

---

[9] Tavard, *The Spiritual Way of St. Jeanne d'Arc*, 47.
[10] Régine Pernoud and Marie-Véronique Clin, *Joan of Arc: Her Story* (New York: St. Martin's Press, 1999), 119.

began to be publicly known. To fulfill her vocation and mission in life, she would thereafter identify herself and be identified by others as Jeanne La Pucelle (Joan the Maid).

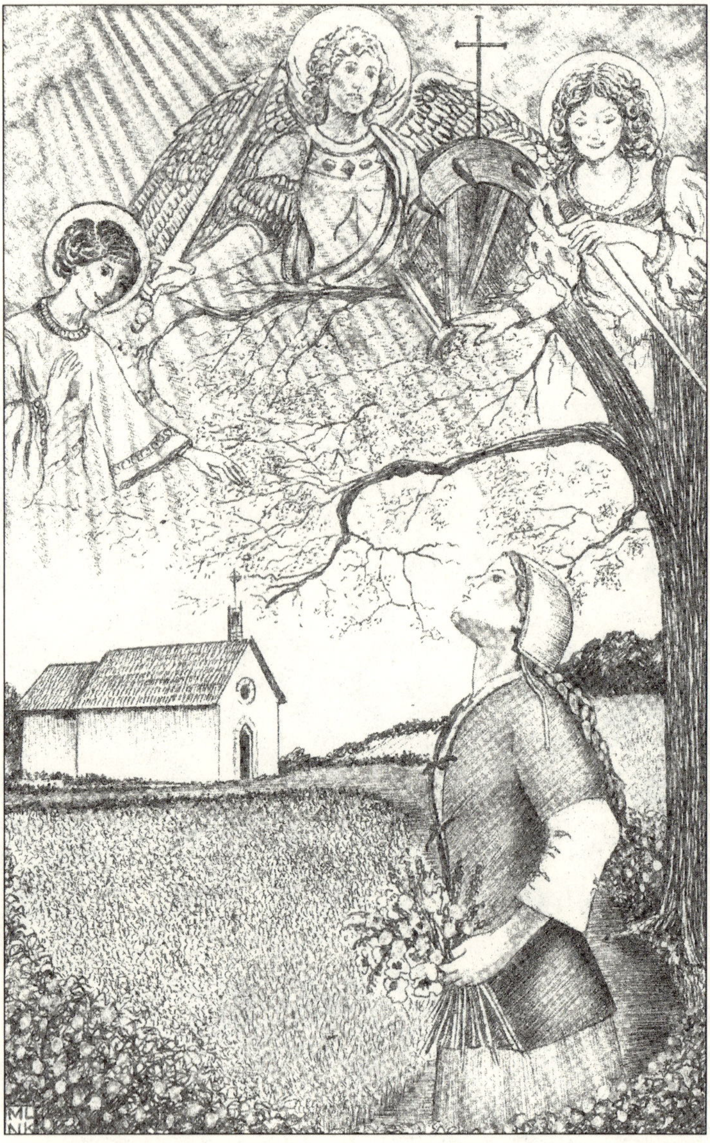
ML
NK

✤ Meditation ✤

A GODLY UPBRINGING

From the beginning of creation and throughout the millennia of human history, God the Creator has revealed the divine plan for human happiness. By creating man male and female in His own image and likeness, our Creator invites a man and a woman together to share in His own life-giving love. God the Creator wills the conjugal union of the two to become one body of persons, capable of procreating new human beings and responsible for forming a new family.

Joan's mother, Isabelle, began the description of her daughter as "born in holy wedlock." In other words, Jacques and Isabelle had entered into holy matrimony, a sacrament of Christ and His Church with sanctifying grace, by which they were partners with God in being faithful and forming a holy family. Theirs was not simply a living arrangement, legally recognized by the civil authorities, to enjoy sexual relations, albeit with moral responsibility for any children conceived and born to them. Their union was a covenant, a lifelong religious commitment, made in the presence of Almighty God and His Church, to bring children into the world and have them baptized and confirmed as children of God and members of Christ's Church.

Joan's parents were quite unlike many of the aristocrats of the time who were unfaithful to their spouses and who fathered or mothered children outside holy wedlock. Isabeau of Bavaria, the wife of King Charles VI, was unfaithful to her husband. And even her son, who became King Charles VII, had an officially recognized mistress, Agnes Sorel, probably after Joan's death, which added to his discredit in the eyes of historians, if not of his peers. Without foreknowledge of her king's future marital infidelities, the imprisoned Jeanne d'Arc would later respond to her trial judges that King Charles was "a good Christian."

A good mother's instruction and a faithful father's protection are invaluable in the rearing of children, particularly in the ways of virtue. Spiritual and moral formation is at least as important for wholesome childhood development into adolescence and responsible adulthood as intellectual education and physical training. Good neighbors and good citizens most often come from good families, in which the love of God and one's fellow men have been instilled since childhood. Wise parental guidance, firm discipline, and the virtuous example of parents in meeting their religious and social responsibilities enable younger generations to mature into godly adults.

Such virtuous training Jeannette received from her parents, Jacques and Isabelle. By having her baptized and confirmed in the Catholic Faith, they gave Jeannette back to God the Father as His own child, His daughter sealed in the Holy Spirit. Then, as she grew in the knowledge and love of God, the heavenly Father revealed His will to her prayerful soul by the repeated Voices of His heavenly emissaries. That vocation to be a "soldier of Christ" and to rally the king and the armies of France to victory became firmer for her from the ages of thirteen to sixteen years.

"Honor your father and your mother" is the Fourth Commandment of God. Yet a reasonable person's first love must necessarily be directed to the one true God, the source of all life, as posited in the first three of the Ten Commandments handed down in the Judeo-Christian tradition from the time of Moses. The last seven Commandments reveal the order of charity and justice toward neighbor and self; and, of course, a child's first neighbor is his mother, then his father and other family members.

The preface to the *Roman Catechism* states the purpose of Christian education: "The whole concern of doctrine and its teaching must be directed to the love that never ends. Whether something is proposed for belief, for hope, or for action, the love of our Lord must always be accessible, so anyone can see that all the works of perfect Christian virtue spring from love and have no other objective than to arrive at love."

The latest *Catechism of the Catholic Church* describes both human and divine virtues: "A virtue is a habitual and firm disposition to do the good. It allows the person not only to perform good acts, but to give his best. The virtuous person tends toward the good with all his sensory and spiritual powers; he pursues the good and chooses it in concrete actions" (no. 1803). Of the human (moral) virtues, which are acquired by human effort, four are cardinal: prudence, justice, fortitude, and temperance" (nos. 1804, 1805). "The human virtues are rooted in the theological virtues, which adapt man's faculties for participation in the divine nature. They dispose Christians to live in a relationship with God the Holy Trinity. They have the One and Triune God for their origin, motive, and object. The theological virtues are the foundation of Christian moral activity.... They inform and give life to all the moral virtues. They are the pledge of the presence and action of the Holy Spirit in the faculties of the human being. There are three theological virtues: faith, hope, and charity" (nos. 1812, 1813). The lives of the saints, such as Joan of Arc, reflect the supreme virtuousness of the one good God.

For the love of God, a child is thus obliged to love and honor father and mother. Joan always honored and obeyed her parents, until she realized that their will for her came into conflict with God's will. As she herself said, her parents watched her very closely during her midteen years. Consequently, she did not tell them of her mission from God and her intention to leave home to pursue the mission among soldiers. They knew only that she had pledged her virginity to God and would not marry any young man they might have had in mind for her.

In her vow of virginity "as long as it pleases God," Joan followed the example of the Blessed Virgin Mother Mary, to whom she was so greatly devoted. Her response to the Holy Spirit's grace was a wholehearted embrace of virginal chastity "for the sake of the kingdom of God" (Matt. 19:12; Luke 18:29), a key evangelical counsel of the Lord Jesus Himself. She understood that her vocation to virginity was necessary to obtain God's special graces to accomplish her unique mission. "This is what defines her and gives her an unmistakable spiritual identity. The littleness of Jeanne and her ensuing self-knowledge as God's daughter is precisely the ground for the virginity connoted by the appellation *la pucelle*."[11] "Jeanne's mission was to be a virgin soul. Only a virgin soul can engage in the struggle for justice without feeling hatred for the unjust, can obtain victory without taking pride in success."[12]

"This French saint ... is particularly close to Saint Catherine of Siena. They are two young women of the people, lay and consecrated in virginity, two committed mystics, not in a cloister, but in the midst of the most dramatic realities of the Church and of the world of their time. They are perhaps the most characteristic examples from among those 'strong women' who, at the end of the Middle Ages, fearlessly took the great light of the Gospel to the complex vicissitudes of history. We could place her next to

---

[11] Tavard, *The Spiritual Way of St. Jeanne d'Arc*, 34.
[12] Ibid., 48.

the holy women who stayed on Calvary, close to Jesus Crucified, and Mary, his Mother."[13]

Thus Joan, a layperson "consecrated in virginity," a committed mystic and confirmed soldier of Christ, kept secret from her parents her intention to follow the heavenly Voices of God's emissaries, the Archangel Michael and the virgin martyrs Catherine of Alexandria and Margaret of Antioch. The light from above would guide her way to understand her mission and strengthen her resolve to accomplish it, despite the trials and tribulations she would face.

> *Hear, O daughter, consider, and incline your ear;*
> *forget your people and your father's house;*
> *and the king will desire your beauty.*
> *Since he is your lord, bow to him.* (Ps. 45:10–11)

---

[13] Pope Benedict XVI, general audience, January 26, 2011.

II

The Religious Patriot

A nation of firm purpose You keep in peace,
in peace for its trust in You.

—Isaiah 26:3 (NAB)

⚜

In Search of the Dauphin

Joan willingly and single-mindedly responded to God's call to become a soldier of Christ and lead the French forces in the just cause of expelling the English invaders. But the teenage girl first had to find the dauphin Charles and then convince him that God Himself willed Charles to be the true heir to his father as king of France and vassal to the King of heaven, Christ Jesus the Lord.

Vaucouleurs was a walled and fortified town, about twenty kilometers north of Domrémy. There lived Robert de Baudricourt, a castellan baron of the area, whom Joan needed as a reference in order to meet the dauphin. So she left Domrémy with her godmother's husband, Durand Laxalt, ostensibly to visit their home in a village near Vaucouleurs. From there she had Laxalt bring her to Baudricourt. Joan informed him that the city of Orléans was under siege by the English and that she must reach the dauphin before Lent in order to lead his army to repulse the enemy from that key city on the Loire River. A delay would mean the loss of Orléans, which could then become the base for the English army's southward march to conquer the rest of

France. "The kingdom of France does not belong to the Dauphin but to the Lord God of heaven. Our Lord wills that the Dauphin shall be made king and have custody of the kingdom, and I shall lead him.... For there is no one [else] on earth able to restore the kingdom of France nor will he [the Dauphin] have any help except through me, although I would prefer to be next to my poor mother, for this is not my station. But it happens that I must go and I must do this, because the Lord wishes me to do this."[14]

Baudricourt mocked La Pucelle's insistent entreaties and told Laxart to "take her home to her father and have him box her ears!" The baron simply could not put faith in a young peasant girl who claimed knowledge of actual battlefield conditions at a distant city and who said that God wanted her to save the kingdom. Not until a couple of weeks later, after word had reached him by messenger from the besieged city, did he realize the accuracy of Joan's prophetic warning about the danger faced by loyalists in Orléans. Only then did he entrust one of his officers, John de Metz, along with an attendant page and some others, including a royal courier, to escort the zealous young woman across several hundred kilometers of hostile territory, to meet the dauphin at Chinon in southwestern France.

From his first conversation with Joan, by her boldness of speech, John de Metz believed in her and her mission. He had heard the widespread prophecy that a young virgin from the eastern frontier would soon save France, previously betrayed by an older woman not native to France. Furthermore, he heard Joan's repeated entreaties to Baudricourt and shared her sense of urgency.

[14] Kelly DeVries, *Joan of Arc: A Military Leader* (Stroud: Sutton, 1999), 41.

She told Henry Royer, whose wife, Catherine, also hosted her in Vaucouleurs, that "she was not afraid of [enemy] soldiers. She had God, her Lord, make a road for her to the lord Dauphin, and that for this purpose she was born." Intrepid indeed was La Pucelle, who instilled great confidence also in her companions. Bertrand de Poulengy, one of four knights of Baudricourt, recalled: "Joan always told [us] not to fear. She never swore ... nor anywhere in her was seen any evil, but she was always such a virtuous girl, just as if she were a saint."[15] John de Metz, giving his testimony in the third person, stated: "The said Maid always told them not to be afraid, because she had done this by commandment. And he believed many things that the Maid said; and he was inflamed by what she said, and as he believed, by a divine love for her."[16] "A divine love for her"—God the Holy Spirit was inspiring pure love for the beautiful, holy Maid in the hearts of those who encountered her!

Joan wore the male clothing given her by Laxalt and de Metz for the long and dangerous horseback journey, which also ensured her inconspicuous appearance among the men with whom she rode. The trek took eleven days through hostile territory in cold weather and a rugged countryside. Despite her small escort, Joan had such trust in God's protection that she stopped as often as possible to attend Mass and visit important shrines, including those in St. Nicholas-de-Port and Ste. Catherine-de-Fierbois. Her only discouragement during the journey to Chinon was not being able to attend daily Mass, because of the danger of discovery of her purpose by Burgundian partisans or of ambush by bandits. "If we could hear the Mass, we would do well," one

---

[15] Ibid., 44.
[16] Ibid., 45.

of her escorts, John de Metz, testified about her. He said "that they stopped only twice for Mass because of the danger. Once it was in the cathedral of Auxerre."[17] Traveling was necessary, of course, to accomplish her mission from God on behalf of king and country but was also an opportunity for her to make a pilgrimage of devotion to Jesus, Mary, and the saints.

They rode mostly by night, stopping only rarely in a friendly town or village for some provisions, while Joan prayed. She consumed very little food and sought no creature comforts for herself. She seemed to her male companions to have unusually great stamina, a strong physical constitution, amazing self-deprivation, and a steely resolve to reach her objective. Her modesty too was noted by her male escorts. "The Maid slept beside us … and as for me, I felt such respect for her that I would not have dared to go near her. And I tell you on my oath that I never had any desire or carnal feelings toward her." Thus John de Metz attested her virtuous character and purity of soul, as well as his own brotherly love for such a remarkable woman as the Maid.

After the arduous journey, the small band reached the royal castle town of Chinon. Joan and her escorts waited for some response from the dauphin's inner circle. After a delay of a couple of days, she was led into a large room where the dauphin and his courtiers were gathered. But Charles was not dressed in his princely attire, having agreed to a charade to test this supposed prophetess, Jeanne La Pucelle. Although he had put a regal robe on one of his courtiers and then stood in more modest clothing amid the crowd of onlookers, Joan followed her angel's lead directly to him, despite never having met Charles or seen any image of him. She knelt down, embraced his feet, and said, "Gentle

---

[17] Tavard, *The Spiritual Way of St. Jeanne d'Arc*, 144.

dauphin, the King of heaven has sent me to you for an army to defeat the siege of Orléans, and lead you to be anointed and crowned as the rightful heir to the kingdom of France, which belongs to the King of heaven."

The grandmaster of the Dauphin's household who witnessed the event reported that Joan said: "Most beloved lord dauphin, I have come and am sent by God to bring help to you and your kingdom." The Augustinian priest, John Pasquerel, who became her confessor and chaplain, said that Joan told him her message to the dauphin was to affirm him as "the true heir to France, the son of a king, and that God had sent [me] to you, to lead you to Reims, so that you might receive your coronation and consecration."

Needless to say, the dauphin and his entourage were greatly surprised by this marvelous encounter. Joan asked to speak with Charles privately; and after their meeting, during which she revealed a secret vow he had made only to God, Charles returned to his courtiers radiant with joy. Alain Chartier, then the dauphin's secretary, wrote that Charles was so joyful at what she said that it was "as if the Holy Ghost had visited him!"[18] Joan spent the next three days in Chinon Castle, lodged next to the chapel of Saint Martin, the former Roman soldier and convert to Christianity who became bishop of Tours. At Chinon she also met a cousin of the dauphin, Duke John d'Alençon, who became one of her most trusted friends.

Examinations

The royal advisers, Regnault de Chartres, archbishop of Reims, and Georges de La Tremoille, Charles's financier, urged Charles

---

[18] DeVries, *Joan of Arc: A Military Leader*, 48–49.

first to send Joan to be examined by a tribunal of distinguished clergy and theologians at Poitiers, before giving her the armed forces she wanted. Two noble women also physically examined her to verify that indeed she was an intact virgin, as claimed. "She was twice examined by women to discover what she was, man or woman, wanton or virgin. She was found to be a woman, and a virgin maid. The women who examined her were, as I have heard, Lady de Gaucourt and Lady de Treves" (ladies of the royal court of Yolanda of Sicily, the dauphin's mother-in-law).[19] Afterward Joan went on to the city of Poitiers with her escorts and submitted to a two- or three-week investigation of her background to test her virtues, her faith, and her motives.

Presiding over the ecclesiastical inquiry was the archbishop of Chartres. The learned theologians cross-examined her with all sorts of spiritual and moral questions designed to expose any possible deceit or derangement on her part. Despite her illiteracy and lack of formal theological training, Joan was never cowed by the high and mighty, neither royalty nor clergy. She answered her examiners with simplicity, candor, and even wittiness. A Dominican theologian, Seguin Seguin, who spoke a distinctly regional dialect, asked Joan whether her Voices spoke French; she replied, "Better than you!" When Seguin asked whether she believed in God, Joan retorted, "Yes, I do; better than you!"[20] Challenged about the need for an army of soldiers, since the Almighty Himself could defeat any enemy, Joan declared boldly,

---

[19] From John Pasquerel's testimony, quoted in Régine Pernoud, *The Retrial of Joan of Arc*, J. M. Cohen, trans. (San Francisco: Ignatius Press, 2007), 182.

[20] Críostóir Ó'Floinn, *Three French Saints: The One Who Led an Army* (Dublin: Columba Press, 2010), 33.

"In the name of God, the men-at-arms will fight, and God will give the victory!"[21]

After their very thorough scrutiny of the teenage girl, the Church tribunal at Poitiers sent a formal letter in March 1429 to the dauphin Charles, unanimously testifying to Joan's good character and her authentic mission from God to gather an army for the liberation of France. The clergymen reached an astounding conclusion and gave a most compelling endorsement of Joan for her religious and patriotic mission:

> The king, in view of the testing carried out on the said Maid, so far as he can, and that no evil is found in her, and considering her answer, which is to give a divine sign at Orléans; seeing her constancy and perseverance in her purpose, and her instantaneous requests to go to Orléans to show there the sign of divine help, must not prevent her from going to Orléans with her men-at-arms, but must have her led there in good faith, trusting in God. For doubting her or dismissing her without appearance of evil, would be to repudiate the Holy Spirit, and render one unworthy of God's help, as Gamaliel stated in a council of Jews regarding the apostles.[22]

"Connected with this early stage of her mission is a letter of one Sire de Rostlaer, written from Lyons on April 22, 1429, which was delivered at Brussels and duly registered, as the manuscript to this day attests, before any of the referred events received

---

[21] Cf. Pernoud and Clin, *Joan of Arc: Her Story*, 29–31.
[22] Timothy Wilson-Smith, *Joan of Arc: Maid, Myth and History* (Gloucester: Sutton Publishing, 2006), 86, quotation from Quicherat, ed., *Procès de condemnation*, vol. 3, 391.

their fulfillment. The Maid, he reports, said 'that she would save Orléans and would compel the English to raise the siege, that she herself in a battle before Orléans would be wounded by a shaft but would not die of it, and that the King, in the course of the coming summer, would be crowned at Reims, together with other things which the King keeps secret.'"[23]

---

[23] Herbert Thurston, *Catholic Encyclopedia* (New York: Appleton, 1910), s.v. "Joan of Arc."

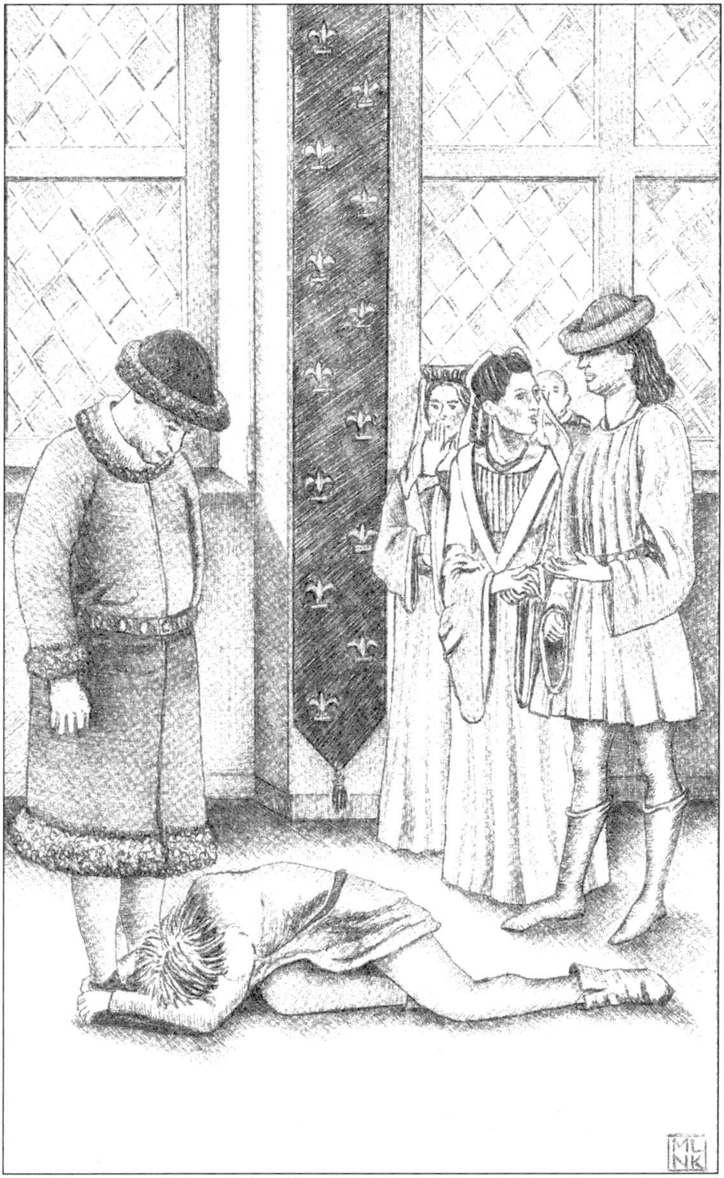
MLNK

✠ Meditation ✠

TRUE RELIGION AND TRUE PATRIOTISM

In God we trust.

—Motto of the United States of America

To the Christians of our days, Joan appears like a pattern of sound, active faith, of submissiveness to a lofty mission, of strength amid ordeals.

—Pope Pius XII

Justice in reference to Almighty God and His divine rights is called the virtue of religion, which describes the bonding of God with His people in a covenant, or sacred agreement. The covenant or religious relationship between the Supreme Being and human beings in the Judeo-Christian tradition of faith is a mutual declaration and practice of faithful love. As God's people have expressed it from Moses' time onward through the centuries of Christ Jesus and His Church: "Hear, O Israel: the Lord our God, the Lord is one; you shall love the Lord your God with all your heart, and with all your soul, and with all your mind, and with all your strength" (Mark 12:29–30; cf. Deut. 6:4–5).

Joan of Arc was certainly "a good Christian" and very religious from her early childhood into adolescence and young adulthood. Her inherent respect for the clergy as religious authorities commissioned by Christ and her devout conduct of daily religious duties were a direct response to the love of God, who was first and foremost in her life. John de Metz added: "Yes, La

Pucelle went most willingly to Mass; she went to confession frequently; she gave alms, very often entrusting money to me to give it in the name of God. As long as I was in her company I knew her to be good, simple, pious, a good Christian, clean-thinking and God-fearing." "Her piety was deep and fervent without being ostentatious or obnoxious: 'Several times,' John d'Alençon testified, 'I saw her receive the Body of Christ; when she saw the host, she shed many tears. She received the holy Eucharist twice a week and she went to Confession often.'"[24] Because of her intense religiosity in prayerful union with God, which showed her "sound, active faith," Joan understood that God willed for her to undertake a lofty mission on behalf of her countrymen. Moreover, she demonstrated real humility in a penitential disposition by frequent sacramental confession, as she herself declared, "One cannot clean one's conscience too much."

The second great commandment of the Judeo-Christian faith tradition is: "You shall love your neighbor as yourself" (Mark 12:31). "Charity in Truth is the principle around which the Church's social doctrine turns, a principle that takes on practical form in the criteria that govern moral action.... Two of these [criteria] are justice and the common good. Every society draws up its own system of justice. Charity goes beyond justice ... but it never lacks justice which prompts us to give the other what is due him.... Justice is inseparable from charity and intrinsic to it. Charity demands justice: recognition and respect for the legitimate rights of individuals and peoples."[25]

Justice in reference to one's fellow men requires respect for their basic human rights and for the common good of society

---

[24] Tavard, *The Spiritual Way of St. Jeanne d'Arc*, 143–144.
[25] Pope Benedict XVI, *Caritas in Veritate* ("Charity in Truth"), no. 13.

and the nation. A person "rightly owes loyalty to the communities of which he is part and respect to those in authority who have charge of the common good."[26] That loyalty to the nation means being not only a law-abiding citizen but also an individual contributor to the common good, even to the defense of society. Loyalty and sacrifice are hallmarks of true patriotism. A religious patriot is a person who loves God and country, upholding the ideals of life, liberty, and justice for all, even to the ultimate self-sacrifice.

Fundamental to her vocation was Joan's "hunger and thirst for justice"; she became one of those whom Jesus pronounced "blessed" during His Sermon on the Mount, "for they will be satisfied" (cf. Matt. 5:6). Joan of Arc showed great patriotism toward her divided nation of France precisely because of her strong, religious love of God and His Church; the bonds of her Catholic religion motivated her patriotic endeavor. Her active faith in the Lord's love for her caused her to submit to a lofty vocation to become His soldier, to receive His "strength amid ordeals," and to undertake her patriotic mission, as leader of the soldiers of France, to liberate her countrymen from the English. "It was a gift of self to the service of justice. She had to fight for justice if she wished to keep her virgin soul."[27]

Yet even though she knew that the English were enemies of the kingdom of France, Joan's patriotic spirit never harbored hatred for them. Despite the alliance of the Burgundians and their vassals with the English, Joan desired to heal the rift between the Duke of Burgundy and Charles VII, so as to bring reconciliation and peace among the warring factions within

---

[26] *Catechism of the Catholic Church*, no. 1880.
[27] Tavard, *The Spiritual Way of St. Jeanne d'Arc*, 143–144.

France and to unify the nation under God's chosen one as king of France. She hoped for a true peace between the two Christian nations, England and France, based on the justice of God and the social justice required of Christian nations. Joan demonstrated by her virtuous character and good conduct that she was a true daughter of God and a true daughter of France. She perfectly fulfilled Christ's exhortation to "love your enemies" (Matt. 5:44).

Joan of Arc beautifully integrated the virtues of religion and patriotism in her own life. By her personal integrity and moral leadership, she effectively communicated the divine motivation of her heart to the Poitiers clergymen and to her men-at-arms, who, after they had reformed their lives according to God's will, would willingly fight for a just cause. Then God would bring them victory for the common good of their country and their king. Joan's extraordinary life and death as a religious patriot, with love for God and country, has become a universal ideal that can be realized by virtuous souls of every nation when they strive for justice and peace in their divine and human relationships. Almighty God's divine rights come first; then the people's human rights follow. Only by devoutly practicing the virtue of right religion can a people of faith become truly virtuous as patriots and together form "one nation under God with liberty and justice for all."

"To the distinguished character of patriot, it should be our highest glory to add the more distinguished character of Christian. Where is the security for property, for reputation, for life, if the sense of religious obligation deserts the oaths? Of all the dispositions and habits which lead to political prosperity, Religion and Morality are indispensable supports. In vain would that man claim the tribute of Patriotism who should labor to subvert these great pillars of human happiness, these firmest props of the duties of men and citizens."[28]

"The highlights of Jeanne's spiritual life are in harmony with the simplicity that is recommended in the '*Imitatio*' [*The Imitation of Christ* by Thomas à Kempis]. Desire for heaven, purity of intention and simplicity of affection, an exclusive devotion to the will of God—all of this nourished by frequent interior dialogues with the Lord were precisely the chief marks of Jeanne's life and prayer: 'I know for certain that our Lord has always been Master of my actions, and that the Enemy [the Devil] has never had any power over me.'"[29]

"The compassion and commitment of the young French peasant girl faced with the suffering of her people became more intense because of her mystical relationship with God. One of the most original aspects of the holiness of this young girl was precisely the connection between mystical experience and political mission. After the years of hidden life and interior maturation, the brief but intense two-year period of her public life followed: a year of action and a year of passion."[30]

---

[28] From President George Washington's Farewell Address.
[29] Tavard, *The Spiritual Way of St. Jeanne d'Arc*, 51.
[30] Pope Benedict XVI, general audience, January 26, 2011.

III

The Holy Warrior

*The Lord goes forth like a soldier,
like a warrior he stirs up his fury;
he cries out, he shouts aloud,
he shows himself mighty against his foes.*

—Isaiah 42:13

*Of a stripling I have made a champion;
over the people I have set a youth.*

—Cf. Psalm 89:19

*Finally, be strong in the Lord and in the strength
of his power. Put on the whole armor of God.*

—Ephesians 6:10, 11

※

Forming (and Reforming) an Army

After the clergy at Poitiers had examined her and strongly endorsed her mission from God, the dauphin Charles entrusted a modest-size armed force of soldiers to Joan's leadership, along with a small retinue of men as her personal staff, and ordered a suit of white armor, a good horse, and other provisions for her. Her staff included the knights John de Metz and Bertrand de Poulengy; her squire, John d'Aulon; her page, Louis de Contes; and her chaplain, Friar John Pasquerel.

The generals loyal to Charles knew that Joan now enjoyed his special favor. Charles could not have given her supreme command of all military forces, since at that time he himself did not command such a national army of France. Soldiers followed their own generals, who were also autonomous aristocrats from various provinces of the country. These military men who had considerable experience of war were the "high command" and remained in charge of combat operations. John the "Bastard of Orléans" was half brother of the imprisoned Duke of Orléans in England and was the principal defender of the besieged city of Orléans. Years later he would be recognized by the widow of his murdered father, fully reconciled and honored with her family, and known as Count John Dunois.

Another was Duke John d'Alençon, a cousin of the dauphin who had met the Maid at Chinon. Joan was very pleased that he was "of the blood royal," and they trusted each other immediately. Thereafter she called him "my fine duke" and pledged to his young wife that he would return safely to her from the battlefields. Other generals of lesser nobility included the constable Arthur de Richemont, count of Brittany; Gilles de Laval, lord of Rais; Poton de Xaintrailles; and Étienne de Vignoles, known as La Hire. La Hire was the bravest, boldest, and most experienced of the generals of war, having achieved in 1427 the most recent of the rare French victories at Montargis, a town sixty kilometers east of Orléans. While he was with the Bastard of Orléans resupplying that town, "La Hire looked up to heaven and delivered this legendary prayer: 'God, I pray that you will do for La Hire today as much as you would like La Hire to do for you, if he was God and you La Hire.'"[31] La Hire, whom Joan repeatedly admonished until he corrected his habit of cursing, later became one of her most admiring and loyal supporters and would have given his own life to save hers.

None of these men ever really relinquished command of troops to Joan, such that they continued to conduct their own military councils. She, however, kept insisting that her divine councils were superior to their human wisdom, military training, and combat experience. Once they had witnessed unexpectedly favorable battlefield conditions that supported her prescient

---

[31] Words of Cousineau, quoted in Stéphane William Gondoin, *The Siege of Orléans and the Loire Campaign, 1428–1429*, trans. Jennifer Meyniel (Paris: Histoire and Collections, 2010), 11.

THE HOLY WARRIOR

observations and had seen the extraordinary trust and readiness of their troops to fight alongside Joan, they gradually deferred to the brilliant counsels from her Voices and implemented her tactics and strategy. Joan very soon became the spiritual and moral leader of all loyal French troops, if not officially commander in chief.

The Maid did not tolerate any female camp followers carousing with her men, or any cursing and blaspheming against the Holy Name of Jesus, including by the coarse La Hire, or drunkenness and disorderly conduct by the troops. In Chinon, as Joan "was going into the royal lodgings that day, a man sitting on his horse near the entrance said, 'Is not that the Maid there?' swearing to God that if he had her for a night she would be no maiden next morning. Then Joan said to the man, 'Oh, in God's name, do you take His name in vain when you are so near your death?' And an hour later that man fell into the river and was drowned. And I tell you this as I heard it from Joan and from several others who said they had been present," her chaplain reported.[32] Her insistence on the soldiers' frequent confession of sins, daily recitation of prayers, and Sunday and holy day attendance at Mass led them to a noticeable reformation of their lives and a renewed commitment to her holy cause. She instilled in them a new spirit of zeal to rally around God's chosen king in waging a just war to liberate the French people from English occupation and to restore peace with honor in a reconciled, reunited nation.

"Jeanne's understanding of herself, her mission, and her relation to the Church was represented pictorially, for everyone to see, on her standards and her flags."[33] Her great standard, the

---

[32] Pernoud, *The Retrial of Joan of Arc*, 182.
[33] Tavard, *The Spiritual Way of St. Jeanne d'Arc*, 99.

flag that she herself would carry into battle, was painted based on instructions from her heavenly Voices.

> The background was white, strewn with fleurs-de-lys. The fleur-de-lys as symbol of the French monarchy ... represents three white feathers, which in the legend of the conversion of Clovis were brought from heaven by a dove to his wife Clotilde. The feathers stood for the theological virtues of faith, hope, and charity, which in Catholic theology are imparted in baptism. At the center of the white field was a painting of Jesus as King of heaven and earth sitting on a throne between two angels and holding the sphere of the world in his hand. The words "Jesus Maria" were written along the side. The standard obviously represented the Lordship of Christ over the kingdom of France, which was one of the basic points of Joan's view of politics.[34]

Joan told her personal chaplain to have a separate standard made, a banner on which was painted an image of the crucified Christ, to rally all the priests who were troop chaplains. Friar John Pasquerel thus assembled the other chaplains twice daily for morning and evening prayers and to sing hymns honoring Christ and His Virgin Mother. "And Joan joined them; but she would not let the soldiers mix with the priests unless they had confessed, [which] she exhorted all the soldiers [to do] in order to come to this gathering. And at the gathering itself all the priests were prepared to hear anyone who wanted to confess." These were further remarks in her chaplain's testimony.[35]

[34] Tavard, *The Spiritual Way of St. Jeanne d'Arc*, 100–101.
[35] Pernoud, *The Retrial of Joan of Arc*, 184.

Joan realized that her soldiers would see a sword as the symbol of leadership in warfare. Marching from Chinon toward Orléans, she received instructions from her Voices to secure a hidden sword at the Church of Saint Catherine de Fierbois. She sent her page to tell the monks that the sword was buried behind a side altar. To their amazement, they dug it up and easily removed the surface rust of several centuries. It had been the weapon of Charles Martel, grandfather of Charlemagne, the first Holy Roman emperor. But Joan loved her standard "forty times better than my sword," she later declared. Like a white knight on horseback, she always scrupulously followed the Christian chivalric tradition of the early Middle Ages. Joan was an anomaly in her own time, since that noble code of honor and justice in the conduct of war was practically extinct in Europe.

Joan's superior moral leadership inspired her soldiers to imitate her virtues and to engage themselves fully in the fight for freedom and justice, according to God's will. Their just cause was the liberation of France and the French people from English occupation of their country: "All those who make war against the said holy kingdom of France make war against King Jesus, King of heaven and of the whole world, my noble and sovereign Lord."[36] Her troops began to believe her own strong conviction that Almighty God was with them and with France and that the Almighty was not pleased with unjust English aggression.

The Holy Spirit inspired the apostle Paul's exhortation to Christians facing danger: "If God is for us, who is against us?" (Rom. 8:31). So too Joan, inspired by God, rallied the forlorn French with a supernatural hope for ultimate victory in the

---

[36] Tavard, *The Spiritual Way of St. Jeanne d'Arc*, 69.

cause of Christ. Their individual morale rose along with their esprit de corps. "When Joan of Arc appeared and they [the patriotic French soldiers] felt her confidence and determination, they followed her with a loyalty which few soldiers in history have given their leaders."[37] "They [the French troops] would have no difficulty in attacking the English, for God was conducting their campaign. If she were not sure that God was conducting their campaign, she would rather keep her sheep [in her father's fields back in Domrémy] than expose herself to dangers like these," acknowledged Duke d'Alençon.[38] The Maid's bold and beautiful spirit had begun to permeate all ranks of troops.

Joan's purity of heart and soul and her virginal chastity always engendered admiration and respect. One after the other, her closest companions in arms, noblemen and commoners alike, marveled at her holiness and at the absence of impure impulses in themselves whenever in her presence. "She was beautiful and shapely," recalled John d'Aulon, her own squire. "Many occasions when helping arm her or other times dressing her wounds, he had seen her breasts or bare legs, but never was his body moved to carnal desire for her, nor did she ever inspire lust in any of her soldiers or squires."[39] Gobert Thibault, the royal esquire, also testified that "in the field she was always with the soldiers. And often when they spoke about the sins of the flesh and used words that might have aroused carnal thoughts, when they saw her and approached her, they could not speak like this anymore, for suddenly their sexual feelings left them."[40]

---

[37] DeVries, *Joan of Arc: A Military Leader*, 30.
[38] Pernoud, *The Retrial of Joan of Arc*, 156.
[39] DeVries, *Joan of Arc: A Military Leader*, 30.
[40] Ibid., 35 (quoting Duparc 1270).

For her part, the Maid began preparing for war by intense training in all aspects of the military art. Although never schooled as a soldier or even as an equestrian, she nevertheless undertook a training regimen that highly developed her skills and greatly impressed her cohorts. "She was most expert in war, as much in carrying the lance as in mustering a force and ordering the ranks, and in laying the guns," reported Duke d'Alençon.[41]

The Battle for Orléans

Orléans was an important city on the Loire River and a heavily fortified stronghold of French Armagnac loyalists. The English objective in besieging the city was to neutralize it and seize control of the entire Loire valley, which was the military frontier between the opposing forces in France. Under English dominance this strategically important valley would secure the lines of communication with occupied Paris, deprive French forces of a key source of income, break the French city as the key symbol of resistance to the English, and jeopardize the dauphin and his kingdom farther south in the region of Bourges. Without capturing Orléans the English forces would be vulnerable to an attack from the rear and the severing of their supply lines to Paris, if they were so foolhardy as to venture south through the vast forests of Sologne with French partisan ambushers along the way to Chinon.

The English regent for France was John of Lancaster, Duke of Bedford and brother to the recently deceased King Henry V. The regent Bedford, acting on behalf of his nephew, the little boy king of England, was also commander in chief of all English soldiers deployed to France. Bedford was married to Anne of

---

[41] Alice Buchan, *Joan of Arc and the Recovery of France* (New York: Macmillan, 1948), 127.

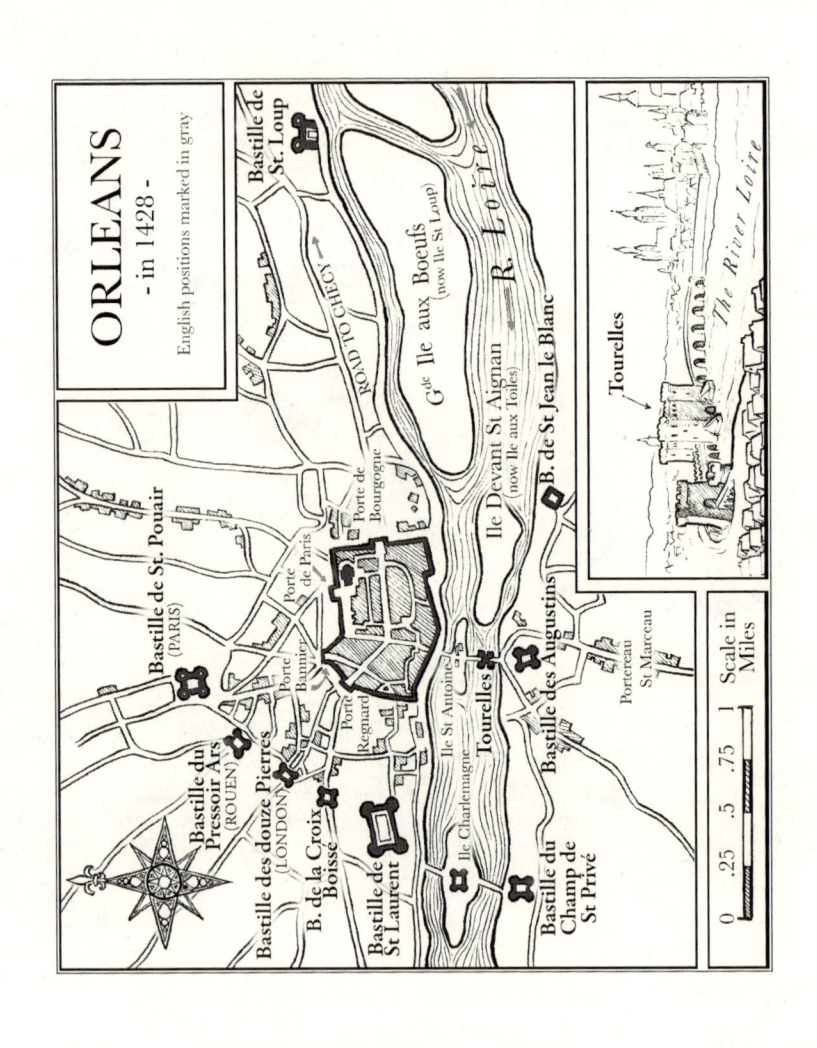

ORLEANS
- in 1428 -
English positions marked in gray

THE HOLY WARRIOR

Burgundy, the sister of Duke Philip of Burgundy, England's main ally. The English captain of war in charge of the Loire campaign was the Earl of Salisbury, who began his advance toward Orléans in the summer of 1428.

Salisbury initiated a series of assaults on smaller towns, including Janville, Meung, and Beaugency, using ruthless tactics such as hanging all who resisted his army. Some French towns surrendered rather than face extermination. The English also spitefully ravaged a nearby Marian shrine church renowned since the thirteenth century. When they reached Orléans in October, the English began establishing their siege fortifications around the city, first at northern and western approaches and on islands in and at the south side of the river at the Augustins, Tourelles, and St. Antoine. A series of skirmishes, attacks, and counterattacks by French defenders ensued over the next several months. During one of them, a projectile hit Salisbury in the face, mortally wounding him. William de La Pole, Earl of Suffolk, assumed command of the siege, leaving a large garrison at the Tourelles led by William Glasdale.[42]

Meanwhile the citizens of Orléans began the awful task of destroying numerous beautiful churches and buildings, mostly on the eastern suburbs of their city, so as to deprive the English troops of living quarters or other permanent shelters for conducting military operations. Since the English were not able at first to seal the city completely, some French resupply convoys did manage to provide occasional relief during the winter months. Despite all their staunch defensive measures, however, the men, women, and children of Orléans faced dire consequences if provisions and reinforcements did not arrive by early spring. The

[42] Gondoin, *The Siege of Orléans and the Loire Campaign*, 28.

English completed their easternmost siege works at Saint-Loup in March 1429, thus restricting French supplies entering Orléans from the east-side Burgundy gate. Panic among local farmers from the eastern villages and fear of traitors from within the city began to grip the people of Orléans. Starvation or surrender seemed to be their only viable alternatives.

On the route to Orléans the Maid inspired local villagers and other armed loyalists to join the convoy or to contribute their livestock and food supplies on that first great march of liberation. An estimated ten to twelve thousand countrymen joined her ranks after the dauphin had commissioned her. At the town of Blois on the Loire, southwest of Orléans, Joan waited a couple of days to ready the relief convoy. She had expected that her troops would then advance along the northern side of the Loire to take the fight directly to the English and defeat all their occupied towns along the way to Orléans, without having to cross the Loire. But the French captains of war, with agreement from the Bastard of Orléans and wanting to avoid close combat with the English, had the army at Blois cross the Loire eastward, then make their way north through the dense forests of the Sologne to the Loire near the English embattlements at the Tourelles and Saint-Jean-le-Blanc on the southern bank of the river.

From her sense of chivalry, Joan's first hope was for a just and peaceful resolution to the Hundred Years' War between France and England. She dictated the now famous letter to the English, which she sent via courier to the enemy commanders in their battlements outside the besieged French city:

Jesus-Maria

King of England, and you, duke of Bedford, you call yourself regent of the kingdom of France; you, William de La

Pole, Sir John Talbot, and you, Sir Thomas of Scales, who call yourself lieutenant of the aforesaid duke of Bedford: render your account to the King of Heaven. Surrender to the Maid, who is sent here from God, the King of Heaven, the keys to all of the good cities that you have taken and violated in France. She has come here from God to proclaim the blood royal. She is entirely ready to make peace, if you are willing to settle accounts with her, provided that you give up France and pay for having occupied her. And those among you, archers, companions-at-arms, gentlemen, and others who are before the city of Orléans: go back to your own countries, for God's sake. And if you do not do so, wait for the word of the Maid who will come to visit you briefly, to your great damage. If you do not do so — I am commander of the armies[43] — and in whatever place I shall meet your French allies, I shall make them leave it, whether they wish to or not; and if they will not obey, I shall have them all killed. I am sent from God, the King of Heaven, to chase you out of all of France, body for body [every last one of you]. And if they wish to obey, I shall have mercy on them. And have no other opinion, for you shall never hold the kingdom of France from God, the King of Heaven, Son of Saint Mary. But King Charles, true heir, will hold it; for God, the King of Heaven, wishes it so and has revealed this through the Maid, and he will enter Paris with a goodly

---

[43] Gondoin quotes from a looser translation of the Maid's letter: instead of "I am commander of the armies," his source translates "I am a warrior and I will confront your soldiers throughout France" (*The Siege of Orléans and the Loire Campaign*, 39).

company.... And in the exchange of blows we shall see who has better right from the King of Heaven. You, duke of Bedford, the Maid prays you and requests that you cause no more destruction. If you will settle your account, you can come to join her company, in which the French will achieve the finest feat ever accomplished in Christendom. And give answer, if you wish to make peace in the city of Orléans; and if indeed you do not do so, be mindful soon of your great damages.

Tuesday of Holy Week, March 22, 1429[44]

She thus afforded the English an opportunity to end their siege and return safely and honorably to England. In going to war and in the conduct of warfare, justice was the governing virtue essential to a true and lasting peace, in the mind of Joan of Arc. But the English contemptuously imprisoned her messenger.

When they departed Blois, where the priests' banner was painted, Joan "had all the priests assembled round [their] standard, and the priests marched in front of the army ... singing the *Veni Creator Spiritus* ["Come, Creator Spirit"] and many other anthems; and they camped that night in the fields and did the same on the night following. And on the third day, they approached Orléans, where the English had mounted their siege works along the Loire bank. The French came so close to the English that the French and English were within view of one another," recalled Friar John Pasquerel.[45]

There Joan met the Bastard, who had come from Orléans to escort the supply convoy and to meet the rumored liberator, the

---

[44] Pernoud and Clin, *Joan of Arc: Her Story*, 33–34.
[45] Ibid., 39.

THE HOLY WARRIOR

Maid. By then she realized the trickery and confronted him, "Are you the Bastard of Orléans? Who advised you to have us come through the Sologne? The counsel of our Lord is wiser than yours or any man's, and also safer and surer!"[46] The French captains had balked at Joan's plan for loading supplies on river barges because of strong headwinds against their direction of movement. But the moment she assured them of her divine counsels, the wind miraculously shifted to a tailwind in favor of the French, whose soldiers loaded the provisions and easily brought their boats to a secure site for passage into the city.

The city militia meanwhile sallied outside to initiate a diversionary nighttime assault on the English position at Saint-Loup. Around eight o'clock at night on April 29, Joan, mounted on a white horse with the Bastard on her left, led the relief convoy through the Burgundy gate, where a jubilant crowd carrying blazing torches met her. In fact, the crowd was so great and pressing in so closely to her that one torchbearer set her banner on fire. She quickly extinguished the flames while expertly calming her terrified horse. "She put out the fire as easily as if she had long war expertise; the men at arms considered this a great marvel."[47] "She was greeted with such joy and applause by all the population, from both men and women, big and small, that it seemed she was an angel from God," reported a local townsman, John Luillier.[48]

The next day Joan sent two more couriers to the English, demanding the return of her first messenger. The Bastard, on his part, threatened the execution of all English prisoners held in Orléans if the enemy refused. The English commander immediately

---

[46] Gondoin, *The Siege of Orléans and the Loire Campaign*, 41.
[47] Pernoud and Clin, *Joan of Arc: Her Story*, 40–41.
[48] Gondoin, *The Siege of Orléans and the Loire Campaign*, 41.

thereafter released the French courier. From within the city, on two successive days, Joan sent messages to the English, one by an arrow, and shouted to Glasdale to surrender and spare their lives or face disaster. And both times Glasdale and his troops cursed her as a witch and an Armagnac whore and said they would burn her if she was captured. She grieved over their impending doom for not heeding her warnings.

On the quiet days of May 2 and May 3, in the midst of appreciative crowds, Joan went around Orléans viewing the English ramparts prior to the upcoming battles. The Bastard had galloped toward Blois to lead the second relief convoy along the route Joan had originally wanted. That convoy, escorted by many of the French troops who had also returned to Blois, arrived on the morning of May 4 near Orléans. Joan, accompanied by La Hire, rode out to meet them, surprisingly without any interference from the English, who remained in their forts. "Serious fighting began in the afternoon with a violent attack on the St.-Loup barbican, during which Joan experienced her first exchange of fire. Hoards of French threw themselves into the assault on the English fortifications and managed to take control of the fortress. They killed ... one hundred forty from the enemy camp and took forty or so prisoners. Talbot's troops ... tried to help their fellow countrymen but ... the [French contingent from Orléans] intercepted their route. The fortress at St.-Loup was lost and it was immediately ransacked and destroyed."[49]

Apparently without consultation with Joan, since they did not view her as their supreme commander, the French war chiefs paused on May 5 to debate their next tactical move against the other English fortifications. Early on May 6 their troops crossed

---

[49] Gondoin, *The Siege of Orléans and the Loire Campaign*, 43.

the Loire by a makeshift bridge, formed by attaching two boats, in an attempt to break the south-bank English fortifications. The French landed near Saint-Jean-le-Blanc and met no resistance because that fortification had been abandoned by the English for being too vulnerable. The French then moved toward the Augustins fortress, but faltered because of timidity, such that the English counterattacked en masse and caused severe French losses. The Maid and La Hire immediately rallied the bravest of their troops from another sector of Orléans, ignoring the orders of the garrison commander, Raoul de Gaucourt, half brother of Regnault de Chartres, who had forbidden anyone from leaving Orléans. The courageous French contingent met the English in close combat, breaking their momentum and forcing them back into the Augustins fortress. After fierce French assaults, the fortress fell, and French prisoners were freed. Joan suffered a foot injury during the attack and returned to the city for treatment. That evening the French prepared siege works of their own against the Tourelles fortress, to which most of the remaining enemy had retreated.

May 7 was the most decisive day in the battle for Orléans. "Joan arose early and prepared for battle as she had every other day during her sojourn at Orléans: she confessed to Jean Pasquerel and heard Mass."[50] She sent for a table and asked the priests to adorn it for the Holy Sacrifice of the Mass; and the priests offered two Masses that morning in the field, which she and the entire army attended with great devotion.[51] She then exhorted her troops for the attack. "Perceval de Cagny wrote:

---

[50] DeVries, *Joan of Arc: A Military Leader*, 86–87.
[51] Cf. Fr. Etienne Robo (New York: Spiritual Book Associates, 1947, 1948), 85.

'The Maid said to those who were with her: By Saint Martin, I will take this [the Tourelles] today and return to the city over this bridge.'"

Early that morning the French troops brought out their ladders to climb the Tourelles fort. Joan led the charge with banner unfurled to inspire her men. "Throughout the day, they scrambled down into the trenches around the barbican, climbed along the walls; they fell, pulled and hit.... Axes, spears, gisarmes, and lead mallets cracked the kettle helmets, ripped open armor, tore the coats of mail and smashed the bassinets. From the right bank the [people of Orléans] constructed a pontoon bridge over the [main] bridge's broken arches and attacked the English from behind."[52] Yet, as she had prophesied days before, Joan was struck by an arrow just above her left breast and fell backward in excruciating pain. She was rushed to the rear; and when word spread of her serious wound, her soldiers panicked and retreated from the Tourelles. The French war chiefs and the Bastard hurried to her side and decided to end the attack until the following day. But after only a brief period, Joan helped remove the arrow from her chest and cried out, "Return under God's Will and attack again, because the English have undoubtedly little force to defend themselves; we can capture them at Tourelles and take control of their barbicans!"[53]

Then mounting her horse, Joan left for a few minutes of prayer and returned, declaring, "Watch for the moment when I place my standard in or against the barbican." After reentering the fray, Joan brought her waving banner to that outer barbican and yelled to the French soldiers, "Enter... for the city is yours!"

[52] Gondoin, *The Siege of Orléans and the Loire Campaign*, 46.
[53] Ibid., 50.

Her men redoubled their intensity and chased the English into the Tourelles fortress itself. "However, the French had floated a fired barge under the drawbridge between the Tourelles and the barbican, [which] caused the weakened drawbridge to collapse under the weight. Many soldiers... plunged into the Loire River. William Glasdale, captain of Tourelles, was among those who drowned."[54] By the evening of May 7 the French completely controlled the Tourelles. Rather than take pleasure with her soldiers in the utter destruction of the Englishmen in the Tourelles, Joan wept for the poor souls of the enemy who had died that day.

The *Journal du Siège d'Orléans* (*Journal of the Siege of Orléans*) described the ecstasy:

> Everyone was filled with a great joy and praised Our Lord for the great victory which He had given them. And well they should have done so, for it is said that this assault, which lasted from the morning all the way to sunset, was so grandly fought and defended. It was one of the most beautiful feats of arms which had been done for a very long time. All of the clergy and the people of Orléans sang devoutly the *Te Deum Laudamus* [You God We Praise], and all of the bells of the city were rung, very humbly thanking Our Lord... for his glorious divine relief. And there was great joy in all parts, giving wondrous praise to their brave defenders, and especially above all to Joan the Maid, who spent the night with her lords, captains, and men-at-arms on the battlefield, to guard the Tourelles which they had bravely conquered.[55]

---

[54] Ibid.
[55] DeVries, *Joan of Arc: A Military Leader*, 91.

On the Sunday morning of May 8, 1429, the English recognized the futility of their siege against Orléans, and abandoned and partially destroyed their last siege works around the city. They decided nevertheless to assemble in field battle formation in front of the city walls, in an attempt to induce the French defenders into open combat. "The French came out ... and matched their battle ready formation. Next to Joan's standard flew the banners of the Marshall de Boussac, Sire de Rais, the Bastard of Orléans, and Florent d'Illiers, La Hire, and Poton de Xaintrailles.... For an hour they took stock of each other."[56] Joan was reluctant to fight on a Sunday but, confident that God would give victory, was ready to do so if the English attacked first. Suffolk, though, backed down and withdrew his English troops to other towns still under English control, such as Meung and Beaugency or Jargeau.

Joyous celebrations on every city street in Orléans continued for two full days, with Holy Masses of thanksgiving, processions, and other festivities. On May 9 the dauphin Charles wrote a letter to all his subjects, commending the bravery of those who sacrificed so much on behalf of king and country; amazingly, though, he did not even mention the role of Joan. The citizens of Orléans thought otherwise:

> It is true that all of the civic and military leaders were heralded for their role in the fight, but no one was praised by the people of Orléans as Joan. She was singled out among all of the others because everyone knew that she was pivotal in determining that this city would not fall to the English. She fought for command from the lack-luster

---

[56] Gondoin, *The Siege of Orléans and the Loire Campaign*, 50.

French military leaders, and she received it. She fought for the allegiance of the French soldiers, and she earned it. She fought for the love of the city's inhabitants, and she gained it. The people would always remember what she had done there early in May 1429.... After she raised the siege of Orléans, Joan was no longer simply "the Maid", La Pucelle. She had become *La Pucelle d'Orléans*, the "Maid of Orléans."[57]

The defeat of the English siege of Orléans, attained through divine assistance, had been the Maid's first objective. The second necessary objective was the city of Reims for the anointing and coronation of Charles VII at the cathedral, the traditional site for the crowning of legitimate kings of France. The first obstacle that Joan faced, however, was not so much the long-distance march there through territory mostly occupied by Burgundian partisans of the English as it was hesitancy by Charles and the French captains of war. One or two captains wanted to proceed immediately into Normandy to recover French control of that province from the English. Yet the number of battle-ready French troops had been greatly depleted to about two thousand men, according to some modern estimates, after their attacks on English fortifications around Orléans. Thus, Joan and the other battle leaders traveled to Loches Castle, where Charles had relocated, to ask for more troops in order to recapture the towns around Orléans and the Loire River valley. Once the Loire valley was secured, the main French army would march on to Reims, where Joan insisted Charles must first receive the divine anointing from Christ's bishop before he could effectively reunite his people.

[57] DeVries, *Joan of Arc: A Military Leader*, 95–96.

The month spent in recruitment bore some fruit, as Charles heeded Joan's incessant entreaties to hasten the mustering of troops. "'He commanded the nobles of all of his lands' to provide men and arms for the army which was 'mustered for the cleaning up of the Loire River.'" Joan had about twelve hundred men-at-arms, plus other infantry, archers, and artillerymen, when she set out for Jargeau, less than twenty kilometers east of Orléans.[58] Other estimates put the total number of French troops, both the combat tested and new recruits, at five to eight thousand men.

"Cleaning Up" the Loire

"For the cleaning up of the Loire River," the French soldiers were now under the supreme command not of Joan but of Duke John d'Alençon, whose leadership was authorized by the dauphin. But for his part, John so trusted Joan that he deferred to her counsels in the course of combat operations. Duke John later recalled that "there was a debate among the captains because some were of the opinion that they should attack the town, and others held a contrary view, maintaining that the English were very powerful and were there in great numbers. When Joan saw that there was discussion between them, she told them to fear no numbers and assured them that they would have no difficulty attacking the English, for God was conducting their campaign."[59] The French troops soon began attacking the suburbs of Jargeau but faltered in the face of an English counterattack until Joan, "picking up her standard, went into the attack, exhorting her soldiers to be of good heart." They

---

[58] DeVries, *Joan of Arc: A Military Leader*, 99.
[59] Pernoud, *The Retrial of Joan of Arc*, 156.

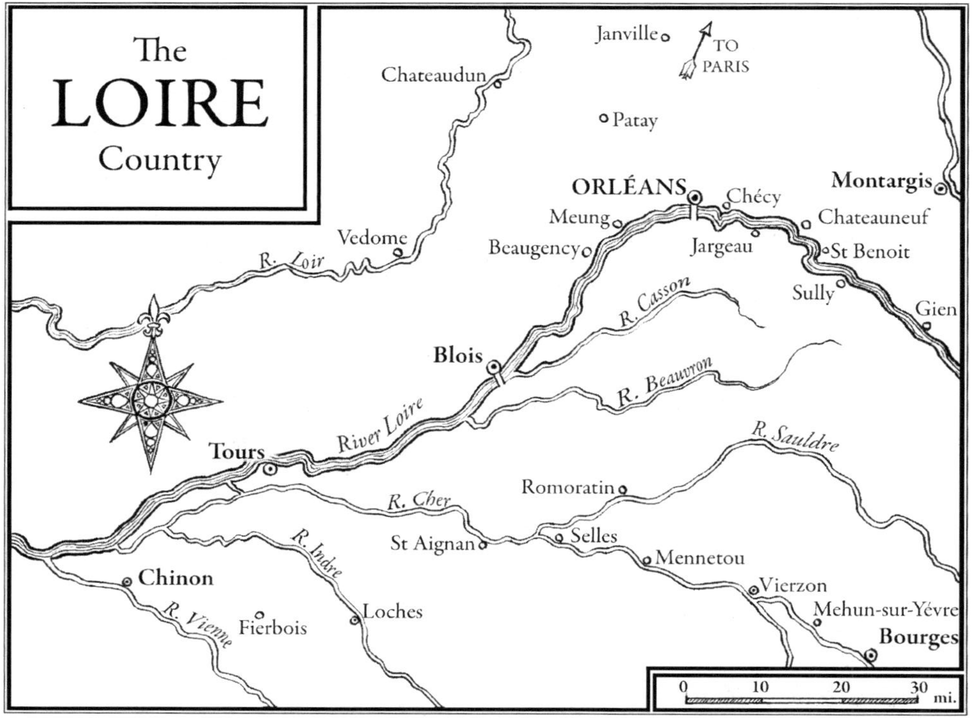
The
LOIRE
Country
Chateaudun
Janville
TO
PARIS
Patay
ORLÉANS
Chécy
Montargis
Meung
Chateauneuf
Vedome
Beaugency
Jargeau
St Benoit
R. Loir
R. Casson
Sully
Gien
Blois
R. Beauvron
River Loire
Tours
R. Sauldre
Romoratin
R. Cher
St Aignan
Selles
Mennetou
R. Indre
Chinon
Vierzon
Loches
Mehun-sur-Yévre
R. Vienne
Fierbois
Bourges
0
10
20
30
mi.

chased the English back into the fortified town of Jargeau and lodged that night in the town's suburbs.

Joan offered the English and the resident townsfolk reasonable terms of surrender or retreat, but they refused, as they had outside Orléans, and the French resumed an intense artillery bombardment. During the attack on Jargeau, in an exchange of cannon fire between the opposing forces, Joan warned John d'Alençon to move away from a location near her so as to avoid an incoming round soon to be fired from an English cannon. "I fell back, and a little later on that very spot where I had been standing, someone [else] was killed. That made me very much afraid, and I wondered greatly at Joan's sayings after all these events," d'Alençon later testified.[60]

Joan and the other captains agreed on a direct assault against Jargeau, although d'Alençon wanted to continue the bombardment longer. Joan encouraged him: "Forward, gentle duke, to the assault! Do not doubt! The time is right when it pleases God. And one ought to act when God wishes. Act and God will act!"

D'Alençon agreed and authorized the fierce attack, which proceeded from many places for three or four hours, with Joan carrying her standard in their midst. "And with the soldiers breaking in," reported d'Alençon, "Joan was on a ladder, holding her standard in her hands, when the standard was struck, and Joan also was struck on the top of her head with a stone which broke on her helmet. She was knocked to the ground; and when she arose, she said to the soldiers: 'Friends, friends, up, up! Our Lord has condemned the English. At this hour they are ours. Have courage!'" Her exhortation inflamed the French troops to ignore English offers to surrender and to press the attack even

[60] DeVries, *Joan of Arc: A Military Leader*, 103.

more vigorously, "and in a short time, the town of Jargeau was taken."[61]

Sadly many English prisoners were executed by the incensed French soldiers and villagers, evidently without the direct knowledge of the Maid. William de La Pole, the English commander of the occupied city, did surrender to save himself; but because he thought it beneath his aristocratic station to surrender to someone less than a knight, La Pole knighted a French squire before giving his own sword to the man.

Celebrations began that night in Jargeau and in Orléans, which heard the good news.

On the Loire River southwest of Orléans were the towns of Meung and Beaugency, still occupied by English troops. At Meung the French did not follow their usual tactic but only attacked and occupied the fortified bridge there, leaving a garrison of their own soldiers on the bridge. "This was done ... so that they would enclose them there and to always stand in the way of any English military activities," according to Jean Chartier. The French capture of the only easy access across the Loire prevented a quick massing of Talbot's and Scales's English troops with those of Fastolf, commander of their reinforcements. French control of the bridge at Meung also inhibited the English forces from easily aiding their fellows in Beaugency. The main body of French troops then bypassed that town on their way to besiege and recapture Beaugency. All the while, Joan and her troops' victories at Orléans and at Jargeau continued to inspire the enlistment of new recruits, both noblemen and commoners, to the French army: "The duke of Alençon and the Maid ... had six or seven thousand soldiers, who had come to reinforce the

---

[61] Ibid., 106.

army: more lords, knights, squires, captains, and valiant men-at-arms," according to the *Journal du Siège d'Orléans*.[62]

The Constable of France, Arthur de Richemont, a very important aristocrat from Brittany, was not initially with the French forces because he had been feuding with Georges de La Tremoille, the dauphin's conniving adviser and financier. The feud seemed to be over Richemont's aggressive strategy of direct combat against the Anglo-Burgundian armies versus Tremoille's approach for an inactive military, seeking a diplomatic truce. The dauphin, siding with Tremoille, forbade his generals to co-operate with Richemont. Nevertheless, the constable, a skilled warrior who had heard of the Maid's inspiring leadership, wanted to fight alongside her and the French because of his prior close friendship with Charles's older brother, the dauphin Louis, whose premature death from an ear infection had enabled Charles to become the new dauphin.

Joan, recognizing the need for more French loyalists, urged d'Alençon to accept the goodwill of Richemont along with his one thousand to twelve hundred soldiers, which he did. Thus the French forces, with their own increased troop strength, could better meet the English in battle and prevent them from re-gaining the initiative in their Loire campaign. According to d'Alençon, Joan approached Richemont and addressed him: "Ah, good Constable, you have not come on my behalf, but, because you have come, you are welcome." Richemont reportedly replied to her: "I do not know if you are from God or not. If you are from God, I do not fear you because God knows my good will. If you are from the Devil, I fear you even less."[63]

---

[62] DeVries, *Joan of Arc: A Military Leader*, 108.
[63] Ibid., 111.

What then transpired at Beaugency was a brilliant application of several principles of war, especially mass and economy of force, feint, and deception, in the conduct of the military art. The French presented a demonstration of force outside the English occupied town and began their psychological operations to persuade Beaugency that English reinforcements under Lord Talbot were not coming to Beaugency's aid. As the English relief force marched toward Meung on the evening of June 14, they stopped about four kilometers north of the town when they saw the large French army and arranged themselves in battle formation for a fight. But Joan declined their proposed battle that night, because she did not want the English inside Beaugency to hear fighting and realize the nearby presence of Talbot's troops.

Since Joan's troops had declined battle, the English relief force went on to Meung and began shelling the French soldiers occupying the bridge to that town. Meanwhile, "to avoid the inevitable attack and massacre, the [English] at Beaugency preferred to negotiate their surrender and have their lives saved, with the right to leave the town with their belongings in exchange for a sum of money. Early in the morning on June 18, the [English] garrison left the town with their heads low."[64] The French ploy thus fooled the separate English forces into leaving Beaugency without a fight and withdrawing their forces from Meung and from the towns approaching Orléans. Otherwise they would risk being surrounded and decimated by the French. They headed northward toward the town of Patay.

The French force soon learned of their enemy's movements and expected that they would meet the English in open battlefield combat. The Duke d'Alençon asked the Maid what should

---

[64] Gondoin, *The Siege of Orléans and the Loire Campaign*, 56.

be done; to which she asked those present with him, "Have you all got good spurs?" They thought she meant to sound retreat, since the French considered the English to be invincible on an open battlefield with their long-range archers. "No, it will be the English who will retreat. They will not be able to defend and will be beaten, and you will need good spurs to chase after them," Joan declared. Emboldened by her words, the French forces proceeded toward Patay, with their vanguard led by La Hire, Poton de Xaintrailles, and others, while Joan, d'Alençon, the Bastard, and Richemont followed with the main body of soldiers. Louis de Contes, the Maid's page, testified that this arrangement of troops did not please Joan because "she wanted to be in charge of the vanguard."[65] She also knew that a speedy pursuit of the English would limit their time to organize battle formations and defensive positions, perhaps also surprise them, and enable her army to exploit their disarray.

In the countryside several kilometers south of the town of Patay, the English lord Fastolf formed his order of battle as a defensive formation. According to John de Waurin, who was present with the English forces, Fastolf

> ordered his vanguard, supplies, artillery, and non-combatants to hide in the woods along the side of where he planned to fight his battle. Talbot then took five hundred elite mounted archers to a location toward the front of the battlefield, between two hedges through which the French would likely pass. These troops were to dismount and try to keep the French from charging the English until after Fastolf had been able to order his main body

---

[65] Gondoin, *The Siege of Orléans and the Loire Campaign*, 58.

and rearguard, also dismounted, for battle some distance to the rear of the archers. Talbot hoped that he and his troops could sneak through the woods in front of Patay ... and return to the main body without a large loss of life.[66]

The excited French cavalrymen, galloping with "good spurs" to their horses in hot pursuit of the English, had lost the element of surprise; but not seeing the nearby hidden archers or the main body farther back, they headed into the planned English ambush. Amazingly, though, "they saw a stag run out of the woods, which made its way toward Patay and crashed into the formation of the English, who made a very loud cry, not knowing that their enemy was so near them. Hearing this cry, the French front-riders were certain that there were the English. So the French sent some of their companions to notify their captains." The English archers then fled into the woods and ran directly into Fastolf's hidden reinforcements, not yet ordered for battle. The captain of the English vanguard, thinking that all was lost and that the archers were in flight, took out his white standard and fled with his men, abandoning the hedges. The English were in total disarray when the main body of the French army arrived on the battlefield. A veritable slaughter ensued: twenty-two hundred English soldiers lost their lives while only three Frenchmen died. Fastolf managed to escape with some of his men, but Talbot, Scales, and many other English captains were captured.[67]

When Joan arrived with the main body, most of the battle had been won by the cavalrymen of La Hire and Xaintrailles, who exploited the English disarray. Viewing the carnage, Joan

---

[66] DeVries, *Joan of Arc: A Military Leader*, 118.
[67] Ibid., 119–120.

wept profusely for the victims, mostly fallen Englishmen. Her extraordinary compassion for the wounded and dying impelled her to comfort and console them. Louis de Contes testified that when she encountered an English prisoner being hit on the head by a Frenchman and left for dead, she immediately dismounted, "holding his head and comforting him as much as she could" and ensuring that the Englishman had confessed.[68]

The March to Reims

The Maid and her revitalized French compatriots had chased the English out of the Loire River valley, causing them to retreat to more secure locations nearer Paris. The French army's march to Reims for the anointing and coronation of Charles VII would be less challenging without the main forces of the English armies. Nonetheless they faced towns and villages where some English troops or their allied armed forces under the Duke of Burgundy and his vassals were garrisoned. Following the astounding victories at Orléans and its environs and then the rout of the main English forces at the battle near Patay, word rapidly spread throughout the countryside that the French army had been reborn and national pride restored under the spiritual, moral, and military leadership of La Pucelle.

It was advisable that the French in cities and towns along the way to Reims, and in Reims itself, expel their English or Burgundian occupiers and pledge their allegiance to Charles VII, who was to receive his royal dignity in Reims very soon. Otherwise,

---

[68] DeVries, *Joan of Arc: A Military Leader*, 121. Note the image of Daniel A. Balan's bronze sculpture *The Pietà of Joan of Arc* (opposite the title page of this book), which portrays Joan's compassion toward her enemy.

those locales would face the same fate as Beaugency, Jargeau, and Patay. Joan herself encouraged the people of Burgundy to return to national loyalty, despite her unsuccessful attempts to reconcile Duke Philip with his cousin the dauphin Charles.

Her letter to one such town, Tournai, written one week after the battle of Patay, survived the centuries:

Jesus Maria

> Gracious loyal Frenchmen of the city of Tournai, the Maid sends you the news that from here in eight days, whether by assault or otherwise, she has chased the English out of every place they held on the River Loire. Many of them are dead or taken prisoners and they are discomfited in battle.... Hold yourselves fast, loyal Frenchmen, I pray you. And I pray and demand that you be ready to come to the anointing of the gracious King Charles at Reims, where we shall soon be; come before us when you hear we are approaching. I commend you to God. May God keep watch over you and give you grace to be able to sustain the good cause of the kingdom of France.[69]

Charles, meanwhile, relocated his entourage to Gien, east of Orléans. Because of Joan, he was confident that his army would secure the remaining territory toward Reims. But his adviser Tremoille, envious of Joan's position of growing fame and peddling his influence also with Duke Philip of Burgundy, tried to steer Charles toward a military adventure into Normandy rather than going to Reims. The Bastard of Orléans later testified about the royal council meeting that he attended, but Joan did not

---

[69] DeVries, *Joan of Arc: A Military Leader*, 125.

attend. "After the Loire victories, the lords of royal blood and captains wished that the king would go to Normandy and not to Reims. But the Maid always was of the opinion that he ought to go to Reims to be consecrated as king; and she added as a reason for her opinion that when the king had been crowned and consecrated, the power of his adversaries would continue to diminish, and that they would not be able to hurt him or his kingdom."[70] After an unusually long delay by Charles in Gien, which greatly annoyed the Maid and caused her to leave Gien and camp out in the field with her soldiers, Joan's position eventually prevailed at court.

With Joan leading the very large army surrounding Charles and his courtiers, the French marched northeastward. Their first stop was Auxerre, which had been under Burgundian control for more than a decade. Negotiations for surrender took three days, but the city administration yielded and the townspeople opened their gates to resupply the French forces. The dauphin forgave all those involved with the English and their Burgundian allies, without shedding a drop of blood. As the army marched past numerous smaller towns and villages, all the people welcomed the French soldiers and the Maid and did homage to the dauphin. The next major stop, the city of Troyes, posed a more difficult challenge. That city was where the treaty disinheriting Charles VII had been signed in 1420 by his demented father, Charles VI, by his vengeful cousin Philip of Burgundy, and by the ambitious Henry V, king of England, five years after Henry's stunning victory at Agincourt. Most of Troyes's citizens had no affection for Charles or any inclination to submit to his rule, since they

---

[70]DeVries, *Joan of Arc: A Military Leader*, 126–127.

enjoyed considerable economic prosperity under English and Burgundian administrators.

Anticipating their antipathy, Joan dictated another letter, which had a threatening tone to it, like her earlier letter to the English at Orléans, and sent it to the people of Troyes. In part, it read, after a customary opening reference to the Holy Names of Jesus and Mary: "Loyal French men, come before King Charles. Do not fail to do so; have no hesitation about your lives and property if you do so. And if you do not do so, I promise and assure you for your lives' sake that with God's aid we shall enter all the cities that should belong to the holy Kingdom; and we will establish a firm peace there, whoever comes against us. I commend you to God. May God protect you, if it pleases Him! Reply soon."[71] On his part, Charles also sent promises of amnesty to the townsfolk.

But when the large French army arrived to camp outside Troyes, they found the gates closed and the drawbridges erect, barring access to the city. Within that town was a garrison of troops numbering about five hundred men, who made a few sorties outside the walls to engage the French troops, until they realized their opponents' far superior numbers and scurried back inside. On the third day, the dauphin called a meeting of his councilors, some of whom wanted to bypass Troyes and proceed to Reims. Joan was called in to give her viewpoint and urged Charles to authorize a siege of the city to ensure its surrender first. When the defenders of Troyes saw Joan organizing the placement of artillery pieces and bundles of wood to fill in the moat, they recognized that devastation would follow. After four days of negotiations between their emissaries and those of the

[71] Ibid., 130.

dauphin, the citizens of Troyes finally realized that there were no English reinforcements coming and that their resistance to the Maid and her dauphin was futile. They surrendered without bloodshed.

No more opposition faced Charles and his forces on the way to Reims. Other villages and the larger town of Châlons on the Marne River warmly greeted the Maid and the dauphin, who had promised amnesty and reconciliation in return for their capitulation to his rule. Joan's repeated entreaties were: "Surrender yourselves to the King of heaven and to gentle King Charles." While at Châlons, Joan was visited by several persons from her home village, including her father and her brothers Peter and John, who thereafter joined her troops. Another of her townsmen, the farmer Gerardin d'Epinal, recalled that before she had left home, Joan had wanted to tell him a secret, but could not because he was a Burgundian sympathizer. Nevertheless, she warmly greeted and spoke with him and his four traveling companions, telling him then that "she feared nothing except treason."[72] Once the army reached Reims, the suddenly hesitant and fearful dauphin began to worry about potential enemies in the city. Joan reassured him: "Do not doubt, as the burgesses of the town of Reims will come to meet with you." And so they did.

Coronation in the Cathedral

The coronation ceremony of King Charles VII began with great solemnity in the magnificent cathedral of Reims on July 16, 1429, officiated by Archbishop Regnault de Chartres, the royal adviser. Although he was the appointed archbishop of Reims, de Chartres had not taken possession of his church during the years Burgundy

---

[72]DeVries, *Joan of Arc: A Military Leader*, 133.

controlled the city. Now he represented Christ the High Priest and King of kings, invoking God's Holy Spirit upon Charles and the assembled people, who overflowed the cathedral into the plaza. The four knights escorting the holy vial entered the church on horseback amid an exuberant throng of people; prelates, bishops, priests, and nobility surrounded Charles. First of all, Charles took the required oath to God, to Christ's Church, and to his nation. Then the cathedral choir sang the *Te Deum*, and de Chartres blessed the royal insignia: a crown, golden spurs, a scepter, and a "hand of justice"—a second scepter sculpted in ivory.

Yet, the essential core of the ritual was the anointing itself.

> The king prostrated himself on the steps of the altar, while the litanies of the saints were chanted. The archbishop, who had prostrated himself at the king's side, marked the king with the holy oil on the head, chest, shoulders, elbows, and wrists. The king, dressed at that point only in his shoes and in a loose shirt, put on a tunic and a coat of silk. Once anointed afresh on his hands, he pulled on gloves; the ring that was the symbol of the union between the king and his people was slipped on his finger. The crown was taken from the altar and placed on the new king's head, but not before ten of the twelve peers of France who were actually present, five laymen and five ecclesiastics, had held it above his head as he was led from the altar up to the dais on which was placed the throne. It was then that, as depicted on the seals of the time, the new king appeared in royal majesty.[73]

---

[73] Pernoud and Clin, *Joan of Arc: Her Story*, 65–66.

Three gentlemen in attendance later reported to King Charles's absent wife, telling her: "And at the hour that the king was consecrated and also when they had placed the crown on his head, every man cried out: 'Noel!' And the trumpets sounded so that it seemed as though the walls of the church should have crumbled. During the aforesaid mystery, the Maid was always at the king's side, holding his standard in her hand. It was fine to see the elegant manners not only of the king but also of the Maid, and God knows that you would have wished them well." The chronicler of the siege of Orléans went further in capturing the general emotion of the scene, after the archbishop and the peers pledged homage and Joan herself went to kneel before the king. "Embracing the new king's legs, she wept, evoking great pity in all who beheld her, and said, 'Gentle king, from this moment the pleasure of God is executed. He wished me to raise the siege of Orléans and bring you to the city of Reims to receive your anointing, which shows that you are the true king and the one to whom the kingdom should belong.'"[74]

The Maid had become an instant celebrity after the French victory at Orléans. Her fame spread almost overnight throughout France and to other parts of Europe, into the Holy Roman Empire, the Southern Low Countries, and the Italian states. Christine de Pisan, Joan's contemporary, who was a well-known poetess, historian, champion of women, and proponent of peace among rivals, sang the Maid's praises:

> In the year one thousand four hundred twenty-nine, the sun began to shine again.... Behold this woman, a simple shepherdess, more valiant than was ever any man at Rome....

[74] Pernoud and Clin, *Joan of Arc: Her Story*, 66.

THE HOLY WARRIOR

> During the siege of Orléans, her force first appeared....
> With great triumph and power, Charles was crowned at
> Reims. Never have we heard speak of so great a marvel.[75]

King Charles VII's secretary, Alain Chartier, writing to an unnamed prince in late July 1429 after the anointing and coronation at Reims, was effusive in his praise of Joan's virtues. After comparing her military prowess and bold leadership to those of Hector, Alexander, Hannibal, and Caesar, he concluded:

> Here is she who seems not to come from anywhere on earth, [and] who seems to be sent from heaven to sustain with her neck and shoulders a fallen France. She raised the king out of the vast abyss onto the harbor and shore by laboring in storms and tempests, and she lifted the spirits of the French to a greater hope. By restraining the ferocity of the English, she excited the bravery of the French; she prohibited the ruin of France; and she extinguished the fires of France. O singular virgin, worthy of all glory, worthy of all praise, worthy of divine honors! You are the honor of the reign; you are the light of the lily; you are the beauty, the glory, not only of France but of all Christendom![76]

Intrigues during the Lull

After the coronation ceremony, festivities within the royal circle of nobles went on in the archbishop's palace, but apparently without Joan in the company of King Charles. Archbishop de Chartres had an attitude of condescension toward the Maid and thought her to be vain because she appreciated the fine clothing

---
[75] Ibid., 70–71.
[76] DeVries, *Joan of Arc: A Military Leader*, 94.

given her to wear at various formal occasions. He chided her for standing with her banner next to her king at his coronation; but she reminded him that because her banner had shared in the toil of battle, it rightly shared in the honor at Charles's anointing. Both de Chartres and Tremoille were her foremost detractors whenever she attempted to advise Charles on matters contrary to their own designs; they convinced him to exclude her from his inner council.

Those two royal advisers were actually negotiating with Duke Philip of Burgundy, one of the peers who should have attended the coronation of Charles, but refused because of the continuing animosity with his royal cousin over the murder of his father. Joan even had sent Philip a letter exhorting him to be reconciled with his king, but he never answered. The other official ecclesiastical peer absent from the Reims ceremony was the bishop of Beauvais, Pierre Cauchon, who with Philip was an eager supporter of the Anglo-Burgundian alliance and an archenemy of the Maid and her king. Counseling Charles to seek a truce with Philip, de Chartres and La Tremoille contradicted Joan's appeal to move quickly toward Paris, the capital city of France, in order to prevent the English under Bedford from reinforcing their defensive garrisons. Charles had badly misplaced his trust.

Failure at Paris

The Maid was eager to move on with the army, but her newly crowned king was not. Joan had rightly interpreted Philip of Burgundy's absence from the coronation as an insult and a sign of bad will toward King Charles, which would bode ill for any real diplomatic breakthrough between the two cousins and their feuding factions. Charles, however, still naively influenced by the conniving Tremoille, agreed to a fifteen-day truce with the Duke of Burgundy. Philip, meanwhile, cunningly deceived Charles into thinking that he would relinquish Paris to him after the truce, whereas he had already agreed to strengthen his alliance with the English and commit his own forces to defend Paris.

On July 21 the French army left Reims and journeyed to Soissons, which surrendered to King Charles, then to Château-Thierry, where Charles granted Joan's village of Domrémy and its adjacent village of Greux a permanent exemption from taxation, the only favor she had ever asked of him. At Provins, René of Anjou, son-in-law of the Duke of Lorraine, joined his men-at-arms to the French army, which marched on to Senlis, north of Paris, camping nearby on August 15. Bedford and the English proposed battle, but the French generals declined. About six thousand French soldiers spent the day staring across at the eight thousand Burgundian and English soldiers. The Maid, accompanied by d'Alençon, taunted the English, hoping they would come out from behind their stakes, ditches, and wagons into open battle, but they would not. At nightfall, the French returned to their encampment, and at daybreak the English departed for Paris.[77]

King Charles too decided to leave for his royal residence in Compiègne, bringing along Joan to fret about not advancing forward into battle. Still influenced by Tremoille, whose brother served the court of Burgundy, and by his archbishop, de Chartres, also in contact with Philip, Charles lingered under the delusion that Philip of Burgundy was sincere in negotiating a truce. He even agreed to surrender the towns near Paris, which his army had taken back from Burgundian control, and also Compiègne, if Philip agreed to a longer truce and reconciliation. Despite his duplicitous advisers, though, he eventually authorized Joan,

---

[77] Cf. Wilson-Smith, *Joan of Arc: Maid, Myth and History*, 46–47.

d'Alençon, La Hire, and other captains of war to proceed toward Paris for a possible assault on the capital city, if all diplomacy failed.[78]

The army arrived on the northern outskirts of Paris at the town of Saint-Denis, named for the first bishop-martyr of Paris and home of the royal abbey, the traditional burial place of the French kings. From their encampments, the French deployed skirmishers to test for weaknesses in the defenses of the outer walls to the city, and Joan herself examined the ramparts. The order to attack, however, awaited the king's arrival. Thirty-six days after his coronation in Reims, Charles finally ordered the assault to begin on September 8. Joan, Marshall Gilles de Rais, and the Lord of Gaucourt attacked the Saint-Honoré Gate, "hoping to grieve and damage the inhabitants of the city of Paris, more by upsetting the people than by power and force of arms," as a clerk, Clement de Fauquembergue, reported.[79] The Parisians were obviously in a state of high anxiety, provoked by the bold psychological operations and vigorous assault tactics of the Maid and her soldiers, who intensified the attack on the city walls also at the Saint-Denis Gate.

Many Parisians probably wanted to surrender to King Charles, but he did nothing whatsoever to win them over to his cause or to inspire his own army. By contrast with her king, Joan demonstrated intrepid leadership. According to Percival de Cagny, another loyal and enthusiastic chronicler of that battle:

> The Maid took her standard in hand and with the first troops entered the ditches toward the swine market. The

---

[78] Cf. Wilson-Smith, *Joan of Arc: Maid, Myth and History*, 48.
[79] Pernoud and Clin, *Joan of Arc: Her Story*, 77.

assault was hard and long; and it was wondrous to hear the noise and the explosion of the cannons and the culverins that those inside the city fired against those outside; and all manner of blows in such great abundance that they were beyond being counted. The assault lasted from about the hour of midday until about the hour of nightfall. After the sun had set, the Maid was hit by a crossbow bolt in her thigh. After being hit, she insisted even more strenuously that everyone should approach the walls so that the place would be taken; but because it was night and she was wounded and the men-at-arms were weary from the day-long assault, the lord of Gaucourt and others came to the Maid and against her will carried her out of the ditch, and so the assault ended.[80]

Despite her wound, Joan went the next day to find her "fine duke" d'Alençon, who had built a bridge in hopes of resuming the offensive against the walls of Paris. But the Dukes of Bar and of Clemont arrived from the king with a royal order to retreat. Charles also directed d'Alençon to destroy the assault bridgework that very night. On September 13, he sent another order, according to Poton de Xaintrailles, to "return to the banks of the Loire, to the great displeasure of the Maid. Those sitting in the council of the court had won out over those performing exploits in the field."[81] But before she left, Joan went to the Basilica of Saint-Denis and offered there at the altar her entire suit of white armor and a sword she had won from a prisoner during the assault.

[80] Pernoud and Clin, *Joan of Arc: Her Story*, 77.
[81] Ibid., 78.

The Maid-Soldier's Twilight

The Maid's devotion to the spiritual hierarchy of saints had been evident in nearly every city, town, and village she entered, especially by her public visits and devotions at churches and shrines. The war cry of French troops, both as an acclamation and as an invocation, had been "*Mont-joie Saint-Denis*" (Mount-Joy Saint Dennis). After the failed assault on Paris and the king's order to retreat, that invocation became muted among the troops and greatly subdued within the Maid. Joan's military exploits and usefulness to King Charles were nearing an end and her irrelevance to him only just beginning. Moreover, she heard less and less clearly from her heavenly Voices. Her vulnerability to the machinations of her detractors increased, along with the indecisiveness of her king. On Tremoille's advice, Charles had signed yet another truce with the Duke of Burgundy—diplomacy amid duplicity!

The next several weeks of the army's inertia greatly disturbed the soul of the Maid. On September 21, 1429, at Gien, Charles disbanded his army, thereby nullifying the very purpose of Joan's military vocation as leader in the liberation of her nation. At the urging of Tremoille, Charles also refused the request of his cousin, Duke d'Alençon, to allow Joan to go with him and his small force to fight the English in Normandy; she never saw her fine duke again once he had departed the king's company. Instead of letting Joan continue as a bold and courageous leader of soldiers, Charles made her a captive of the court, separating her also from the other two of her closest captains of war, the Bastard and La Hire. Not permitting her to return quietly to Domrémy, the king instead took the Maid with him to Bourges, one of his castle cities; and the trial of her patience began.

If she could not be a warrior, the Maid could still be holy. While residing at the house of Marguerite La Touroulde, one of the queen's ladies-in-waiting, she went frequently to Mass, received the sacraments, and invited her hostess to attend early morning prayers with her. Also, "she was generous with her almsgiving, and most willingly gave to the needy and the poor, saying that she had been sent for [their] consolation." Her reputation for holiness grew, such that "women came to the house while Joan was staying there. They brought rosaries and other objects of piety so that she might touch them. This made her laugh and say to me, 'Touch them yourself; they will be as good from your touch as they would be from mine.'"[82] Joan's humility, neither seeking the adulation of others nor claiming priestly powers of her own, and her charity toward the poor and the afflicted were signs of her genuine sanctity.

Finally it became obvious to King Charles that Philip of Burgundy had been dishonest in diplomacy. Instead of relinquishing Paris, the capital city of France, to Charles, Philip solidified his alliance with the English. Since Bedford was married to Anne of Burgundy, the duke's own sister, the English regent named his brother-in-law Philip lieutenant general of France. In another intrigue, Charles's adviser Tremoille was harboring a personal vendetta against the powerful brigand Perrinet Gressart, who had captured the towns of Saint-Pierre and La Charité on behalf of the Duke of Burgundy in 1423 and then kidnapped Tremoille in 1425 for a huge ransom. Tremoille had been negotiating with Philip primarily to regain his ransom money and his lands, not because of any real patriotic desire for reconciliation and peace

---

[82] Siobhan Nash-Marshall, *Joan of Arc: A Spiritual Biography* (New York: Crossroad, 1999), 119.

between King Charles and his cousin Philip. The deepened ties between Philip and Bedford thus dealt Tremoille a serious setback to his own self-interests.

King Charles, recognizing Philip's duplicity, also wanted to repossess the towns and cities he had in good faith given to Duke Philip in exchange for the capital city. So the king decided to reequip Joan with a small force of men and some ammunition and provisions to retake those towns. But Tremoille convinced the gullible King Charles not to give Joan too big an army for a spectacular victory against Burgundy and England. Tremoille did not want Joan to regain Charles's confidence and displace him from the king's inner circle. The king allowed Tremoille to send his brother-in-law, Charles d'Albret, on Joan's military campaign to report on her actions—in other words, to spy on her.[83]

The Maid left Bourges for Saint-Pierre in late October 1429 with her small force, woefully underequipped and undermanned. The first attack on the town failed, but thanks again to the Maid's extraordinary courage—and divine assistance—the second assault won the battle. Her page, John d'Aulon, recalled the astounding scene:

> Because of the great number of soldiers in the town and its great strength ... the French were forced to retire. At that moment I came up ... I saw that the Maid had been left with a very small company of her own men and others, and I had no doubt she would come to some harm. So I mounted a horse and rushed toward her. I asked her what she was doing alone there like that, and why she had not

---

[83] Nash-Marshall, *Joan of Arc: A Spiritual Biography*, 120–121.

retreated with the rest. After taking her helmet off, she responded that she was not at all alone—that she had fifty thousand men in her company and that she would not leave the spot until she had taken the town. Whatever she might have said, she did not have more than four or five men with her. I know this for sure, as do several other men who also saw her.... She shouted, "Sticks and branches, everyone, so that we can make a bridge!" The entire thing completely astonished me, for the town was immediately taken by assault.[84]

What her page could not see, but what the Maid and the terrified enemy defenders of the town could see, was an army of God's angels fighting on her behalf. For every one of the five stalwart French soldiers with Joan, there were ten thousand holy angels covering his back! The other French troops, also unaware of their heavenly protectors, rallied to the Maid and began streaming into the town, intending to pillage and plunder it.

But Joan absolutely forbade any violence, as Reginald Thierry later testified: "When the town of Saint-Pierre-le-Moutier was captured by assault, where she was, the soldiers wished to do violence to the church and to steal the holy relics and other goods stored there. But Joan strongly prohibited this and defended the place, nor did she ever allow anything to be stolen."[85]

La Charité was a different story. Joan received no heavenly guidance or angelic help for a siege there; so instead of marching northward to La Charité, the Maid ordered her depleted

---

[84] Ibid., 121.
[85] DeVries, *Joan of Arc: A Military Leader*, 162.

forces southward to the smaller town of Moulins. From there she sent appeals for support to friendly towns: Riom sent weapons, Clermont-Ferrand delivered saltpeter, and the city of Orléans, which she had liberated most amazingly, expressed their undying gratitude with money, clothes, and a gunner. Yet all those provisions still did not suffice; so after a frustrating month into a very cold December trying to take La Charité, she abandoned the siege and departed in extreme displeasure.

Upon her return to Jargeau on Christmas Day 1429, Joan learned that she and her family, on both male and female lines, had been ennobled by King Charles, receiving the surname Du Lys, a reference to the royal emblem, the fleur-de-lis. King Charles endowed the d'Arc family with nobility status perhaps in gratitude for Joan's heroic efforts on his behalf and also to free her to go her own way, far from his inner circle of courtiers. Aristocrats of that era could conduct their own military operations, at their own expense, without direct orders from the king, while swearing loyalty to him.

Hence, Joan spent the next several months into 1430 writing letters of support or admonition, depending on the addressees, and visiting some of the cities she liberated. For instance, in January 1430, records indicate she visited Orléans as a show of support when the Burgundians threatened to retake the city; and in March she wrote the citizens there with further reassurances that her soldiers would support them. The Maid or her chaplain even wrote to the violently rebellious and heretical followers of Jan Hus in Bohemia, threatening them with armed force if they persisted in their insurrection against the Church and rejection of Christian doctrine: "If I don't hear soon that you have mended your ways, that you have returned to the bosom of the Church, I may just leave the English and turn against you, to eradicate the dreadful superstition with my iron blade and to snatch you from heresy, or from life itself."[86]

Meanwhile the arrogant Duke of Burgundy took full advantage of Charles's gullibility in making the truce with him through Tremoille. He celebrated "his third marriage with extravagant pomp at Bruges on January 10, 1430. Described as the richest prince in Christendom, he had three wives, twenty-four mistresses, and the rather moderate allowance of sixteen illegitimate children to his credit.... For eight days and nights the city of Bruges excelled itself in display: seventeen nations, who had banking houses in the Flemish city, vied with one another in magnificence; the burghers vied with the nobles so that feast succeeded feast, the streets were hung with the richest tapestries of Flanders, and wine ran night and day from fountains."[87] Opulence, profligacy, chicanery, and hypocrisy aptly characterized that ignoble duke, Philip "the Good" of Burgundy!

By stark contrast, the self-disciplined, abstemious Maid, always loyal to her king but longing for action, was primed for any battle, anywhere, for God and country. With a small band of about 150 men, she set out for Melun. Other captains of war with their men-at-arms joined her: Bartolomeo Baretta from Piedmont with two hundred soldiers; Louis de Bourbon; Kennedy, the Scottish captain with his small contingent; and several others expanded the French forces, although without support from King Charles. Once the Maid had arrived at Melun, the citizens expelled the Burgundian garrison; but she had no consolation there, because her Voices told her that she would be

---

[86] Nash-Marshall, *Joan of Arc: A Spiritual Biography*, 123.
[87] Victoria Sackville-West, *Saint Joan of Arc* (Garden City, NY: Country Life Press, 1936), 250.

captured before June 24, the feast of Saint John the Baptist. The thought of capture by the English or their allies terrified her, so she asked for a quick death rather than lose her freedom at enemy hands.

At the town of Lagny, after three fierce assaults and a considerable loss of men, Joan's troops prevailed and captured Franquet d'Arras, a rogue mercenary allied with the Burgundians and wanted for murder, theft, and treachery. Joan at first wished to exchange him for a French prisoner; but once she learned that the prisoner had been executed by the English, she turned d'Arras over to the court at Senlis, where he was executed for his crimes. Also at Lagny the mystical sword of Charlemagne's grandfather, found at Fierbois, had its last use by Joan—according to popular lore—when she broke it across the back of a courtesan attempting to consort with her troops! Upon hearing about the incident, her king was displeased and remarked that she should have used a stick instead. The chronicler, John Chartier, concluded that, because the blacksmiths of the town found it impossible to repair, the sword indeed had a divine origin.[88] Perhaps that irreparably broken sword was also a symbol that the Maid would soon no longer be leading her anointed king's army.

Another amazing incident occurred at Lagny. Several women asked Joan to pray for a stillborn child, dead for three days. The mother had carried the baby into the abbey church of Saint-Pierre and placed the dead, blackened body in front of an image of the Virgin Mother Mary, in the hope the baby would revive long enough for Baptism. Joan went with them into the church, joined the mother, "prayed, and finally life appeared in the child, which yawned three times and was then baptized. Then it died,

---

[88] Sackville-West, *Saint Joan of Arc*, 254.

and was buried in consecrated ground."[89] News of the Maid's miraculous deeds quickly spread far beyond that town and region.

Even in England the legend of the miraculous Maid had grown so much since the French victory at Orléans that many Englishmen, fearing her supernatural powers, refused to enlist for the war against France. The regent Bedford twice sent threatening letters to officials in England demanding a mandatory conscription of soldiers. Bedford then ordered a perfidy that exceeded even the treachery of the Duke of Burgundy. The pope had authorized churches throughout Christendom to levy special tithes to pay soldiers mustered for Bohemia to quell the violent rebellion of the followers of Jan Hus; the pope himself had sent a considerable monetary contribution for that purpose. Bedford, with the collusion of his uncle, Cardinal Beaufort of England, misappropriated the money in order to pay for his sizable contingent of forcibly conscripted soldiers and then diverted those troops to France for his military campaign against Charles, instead of for the pope's purposes. Bedford's rabid obsession was to eliminate the French Maid and discredit her king by any and every means possible, without regard to Christian principles or papal priorities.

By early May, the combined armies of England, Burgundy, and Luxembourg were advancing toward the fortified and loyal French city of Compiègne. When reports of these massed enemy forces on the march reached Joan, she hurried with her 450 men to help in the city's defense, since its citizens had sworn fealty to King Charles and steadfastly refused to surrender to the foreigners. Several nearby towns had already succumbed to the overwhelming numbers of Anglo-Burgundian soldiers. On May

---

[89] Nash-Marshall, *Joan of Arc: A Spiritual Biography*, 125.

14 Joan staged a surprise attack on Pont-l'Évêque, a few kilometers north of Compiègne, in order to control the bridge over the Oise River and stop the advance by the enemy. Although the initial attack succeeded, the Burgundian soldiers guarding the bridge received reinforcements, such that the French lost control of that bridge.

Two days later Joan planned another surprise attack on the English in Choisy by circling around them from the rear. This meant passing through the town of Soissons, which had also sworn loyalty to Charles during his post-coronation march toward Paris. She rode with her trusted friend Poton de Xaintrailles and with the untrustworthy archbishop Regnault de Chartres for the last time. But, when Joan led her small force there, the townsmen of Soissons, having betrayed their oath to King Charles and realigned themselves with the Anglo-Burgundians, refused passage to the Maid's men, causing her to cancel her plans and move on to Crépy. Despite the city's being almost surrounded by enemy soldiers and against her own soldiers' strong protests about going there, Joan's sense of duty to the loyal people of Compiègne caused her to ignore the obvious danger and rush back to the city. Early on May 23 the Maid safely entered Compiègne; and by that afternoon she launched one last surprise attack against the Burgundians at Margny, directly north of the city. The enemy defenders were completely routed and tried desperately to reassemble for battle. Fortunately for them, the Count de Ligny, John of Luxembourg, a vassal of Duke Philip of Burgundy, while surveying the area nearby, heard the din and came to their rescue, forcing Joan's troops back toward the Notre Dame Gate into Compiègne, with its bridge.

Twice the Maid's troops pushed the Luxembourgers and the Burgundians away from the gate and its bridge; but the third time, with English reinforcements also arriving on the battlefield, Joan could not stop her soldiers from retreating back into the city. Instead, she and a handful of her most loyal and gallant men, d'Aulon and his brother Poton, Joan's own brother Pierre and a few others, covered their comrades' retreat, and once again pushed the combined enemy forces away from the Notre Dame Gate. The governor of Compiègne, Bertrand de Flavy, half brother of Archbishop de Chartres, ordered the raising of the inner bridge, to close the main gate—both to its enemies and to its liberator. Surrounded by her enemies but still trying to fight free, Joan was yanked from her horse by an archer under Lionel, the Bastard of Wandomme, from Luxembourg. At about six o'clock in the evening on May 23, 1430, Joan surrendered herself to the knight, Lionel Wandomme.

The Maid had made a last valiant attempt to protect her retreating soldiers at Compiègne. Her capture outside the closed gates of that city adds to the mystery of her betrayal. Why did not the garrison commander de Flavy send a reserve force to counterattack and repulse the enemy forces and rescue the Maid? Since only the temporary outer bridge was threatened, why did he not wait a little longer to raise the main bridge over the moat so as to enable Joan's safe return, while still protecting the citizens within the fortified city with the retreated French soldiers? Was Joan also imprudent and even reckless by placing herself and her soldiers in harm's way against overwhelming enemy forces? And why did King Charles send Joan on a mission without the necessary forces and supplies to accomplish it? Only God knows the complete answers.

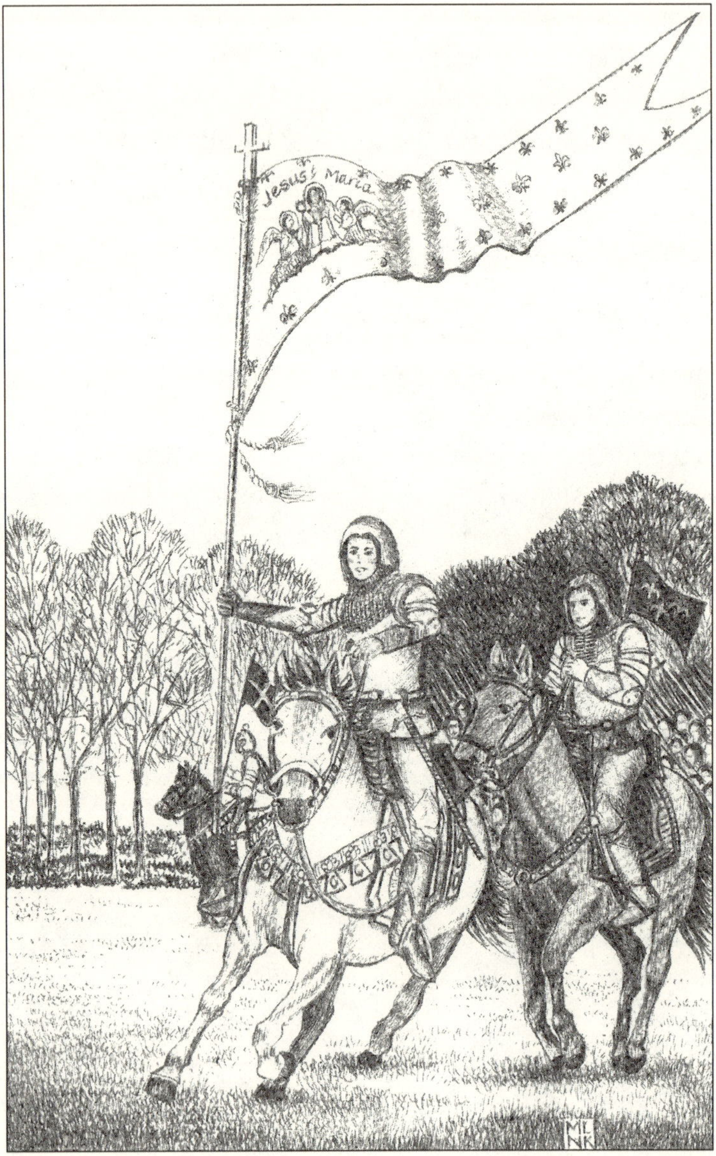
Jesus Maria

THE HOLY WARRIOR

✣ Meditation ✣

THE SAINTLY SOLDIER IN A JUST WAR

A soldier's heart, a soldier's spirit, a soldier's soul is everything. If the soldier's soul fails, he will fail himself, his unit, and his country in the end. . . . Military power wins battles, but spiritual power wins wars.
—George C. Marshall, U.S. Army General

A soldier is someone trained in the military art to be an integral member of a disciplined, organized unit within the armed forces that defend a nation. But a saintly soldier is more than one who loves only his own countrymen while hating and seeking to destroy the enemy. The saintly soldier is a holy warrior, with personal integrity, who fights for justice, for relief of the oppressed, for human rights and dignity, and even for the rights of God as Supreme Ruler over humanity. Saintly soldier-leaders and their holy warriors seek to restore a just order in society with peace at home and abroad.

The first book of Samuel in the Old Testament illustrates several characteristic virtues of a holy warrior in the story of the young man David. First was his love for God and his purity of heart in his earlier years, such that God instructed the prophet Samuel to anoint David rather than any of his seven older brothers. Then David, on behalf of King Saul, fought against the Philistine Goliath, who cursed the God of Israel. David won the victory after slinging just one stone into the Philistine giant's forehead, not because of David's own personal prowess with a sling or any weapon of war, but because of his total trust in the one true God and by the power of God's Holy Name.

Later, while fleeing the murderous advances of the jealous King Saul, who had become his enemy, David nevertheless respected the authority of God's anointed king and refused to kill Saul in self-defense or allow his men to do so. David entrusted his present and future safety to the Lord God. Then, when David and his men sought refuge and asked for food from the priest, he replied, "I have no ordinary bread on hand, only holy bread. If the men have abstained from women, you may eat some of that." David said, "We have indeed been segregated from women as on previous occasions. Whenever I go on a journey, all the young men are consecrated—even for a secular journey. All the more so today, when they are consecrated at arms!" (1 Sam. 21:5–6, NAB). "Consecrated at arms" meant that they carried their weapons in a just cause or a holy endeavor favored by God Himself. They were allowed to eat the holy bread, normally reserved only for priests, because they had abstained from sexual relations for a journey of justice, as pleased the Almighty.

In Judeo-Christian tradition the profession of arms has been viewed as a noble vocation precisely because God wills that the innocent be protected from the wicked and that unjust aggressors be repulsed. Moses' exhortation to the Israelites, "Be holy, for the Lord your God is holy," applied to everyone and to the whole community, including soldiers. True faith in God was both an individual and a communal profession. The nobility of soul exemplified in the young warrior David has manifested itself time and again in later generations of Jewish and Christian soldiers' doing God's will.

In the first century of the Christian era, many sought John the Baptist at the Jordan River: to hear his preaching, gain his counsels, and receive the baptism of repentance. Among the many were military men: "Soldiers also asked him, 'And we, what shall we do?' And he said to them, 'Rob no one by violence or by false accusation, and be content with your wages'" (Luke 3:14). In the Gospels we learn that the Lord Jesus Christ extolled a Roman centurion for his humility, his good character, his generosity, and his extraordinary faith. "[H]e loves our nation, and he built us our synagogue," the disciples had informed Jesus. The centurion then said, "Lord, do not trouble yourself, for I am not worthy to have you come under my roof; therefore I did not presume to come to you. But say the word, and let my servant be healed. For I am a man set under authority, with soldiers under me." The Lord Jesus Christ then declared to his Jewish disciples, "I tell you, not even in Israel have I found such faith" (Luke 7:5–9). On his way home, the Roman captain was told that his servant had been healed at the very time Jesus had spoken!

Many of the early Christian martyrs were soldiers, such as Saint Maurice. In A.D. 287, as commander of a legion of Christian soldiers from Thebes in Upper Egypt, Maurice led his men in refusing to worship pagan Roman gods or to kill innocent civilians in the Roman army battles against the Gauls. Hence the Roman commanding general ordered the Theban Legion to be decimated twice in Maurice's sight. When they still did not compromise their faith or their integrity, he ordered all of them to be butchered, including Maurice.

In the early Middle Ages a code of chivalry developed to apply Christian teaching about declaring and waging a just war with honor, especially if the two warring nations happened to profess Christianity. Medieval orders of Christian knights pledged themselves to God and the Church, striving to live virtuously by a code of conduct. Chivalric values included loyalty, piety, bravery, honor, assistance to the poor, contempt of death, and respect for the Church.

By the time of Joan of Arc, during the Hundred Years' War, however, chivalric ideals were virtually extinct in Europe, except in the heart and soul of the Maid and in those she inspired with devotion to her holy endeavor. "The fact was that the siege of Orléans was made at the cost of flouting the most sacred rules of feudal chivalry. The siege was unfair to its lord (imprisoned in England), unjust to its people, and destructive of the proper order of society in the kingdom of France. The campaign in which it fit was, though Joan could not have known that, the first of the imperialist wars of modern Europe."[90] "She became a warrior, but a most unusual one, who did not use her sword or her hatchet in battle, who prayed for her enemies and who tried to help the wounded among them."[91] Joan insisted on the highest moral standards in conducting military operations. "She absolutely prohibited her soldiers from plundering for their food the local communities through which they marched. Her intent was to unite the French under King Charles VII. Thus the prohibition of plunder engendered good will among the populous."[92]

"Joan of Arc was a soldier, plain and simple. That understood, Joan's other characteristics are also explained. But, what is more, if one can understand Joan's military purpose and character, so too can one understand France's reversal of the Hundred Years' War, which can be dated effectively from her military advent in 1429."[93] Yet, the motivation for her patriotic military endeavors can be fully explained only by her Christian character and religious zeal. Consequently, Joan's first tasks were the elimination

[90] Tavard, *The Spiritual Way of St. Jeanne d'Arc*, 43.
[91] Ibid.
[92] Stephen W. Richey, *Joan of Arc: The Warrior Saint* (Westport, CT: Praeger, 2003), 39.
[93] DeVries, *Joan of Arc: A Military Leader*, 3.

of vices among her troops and the flourishing of virtues in their character and conduct. "Joan had the power to make thousands of armed men love her, not as an object of romantic desire, but as the living focus of their hunger to serve a higher cause. Whenever Joan rose in her stirrups to shout 'Let all who love me—follow me!' she was exploiting a special relationship between leader and led that is unique in all history."[94]

"Character means having the courage of one's beliefs to do and say what is right. Character combined with ability makes the great captain [of war] and is the bedrock of leadership."[95] Joan of Arc's leadership ability was also evident in her mastery of the principles of war, including initiative in combat operations to accomplish major objectives, unity of command, surprise, security, simplicity, mass and economy of force, fire and maneuver, maintenance of morale and esprit de corps and of logistics and lines of communication. "Joan was the practitioner of maintenance of morale par excellence. She is without peer in all military history for her mastery of this principle of war. Her inspirational heroics at Tourelles and elsewhere are an example for commanders of any era."[96] "Duty, Honor, Country: Those three hallowed words reverently dictate what you ought to be, what you can be, what you will be!"[97] "How did she turn the tide of the Hundred Years War in only a little more than one year? Joan was sent from God ... for with that divine mission and by her confident and direct military tactics, combined with her willingness to risk

---

[94] Richey, *Joan of Arc: The Warrior Saint*, 112–113.
[95] William A. Cohen, *Wisdom of the Generals* (Paramus, NJ: Prentice Hall, 2000), 27.
[96] Richey, *Joan of Arc: The Warrior Saint*, 92–98.
[97] General Douglas MacArthur, Farewell Address, United States Military Academy, 1962.

everything, Joan put military aggressiveness into an army that had been forced into a psychology of defeat."[98]

"Already as a young girl, Joan had been [inspired] by the attitude with which Saints Catherine and Margaret confronted the brutality of the world. At Patay she did not share in the intoxication of joy over the victory, but from her charger looked with compassion on her enemies. This was the same woman, who a little while before, cried out that even if the English were to flee as far as the clouds, she would catch up with them.... The picture is one of eternal beauty. When one day there is an end to killing and the hour of the final judgment approaches, the true direction of the main highway of Western history will be made clear: A Maid kneeling at the roadside, while around her echo the whinny of horses and the shrieks of the murdered. She presses the head of an unknown, dying enemy to her breast and prays for his soul."[99]

The natural moral law and Christian doctrine on war and peace require that leaders of nations weigh the moral principles of justice, respect for human life and property, diplomacy, prospects of success, and proportionality of means before declaring war and in conducting warfare:

> All citizens and all governments are obliged to work for the avoidance of war. [But] "as long as the danger of war persists ... governments cannot be denied the right of lawful self-defense, once all peace efforts have failed." The strict conditions for legitimate defense by military

---

[98] DeVries, *Joan of Arc: A Military Leader*, 3–4.
[99] Sven Stolpe, *The Maid of Orléans*, trans. Edwin Lewenhaupt (New York: Pantheon, 1956), 146. Note photograph opposite the title page of this book.

force require rigorous consideration: 1) the damage inflicted by the aggressor on the nation or community of nations must be lasting, grave, and certain; 2) all other means of putting an end to it must have been shown to be impractical or ineffective; 3) there must be serious prospects of success; 4) the use of arms must not produce evils and disorders graver than the evil to be eliminated. These are the traditional elements enumerated in what is called the "just war" doctrine. The evaluation of these conditions for moral legitimacy belongs to the prudential judgment of those who have responsibility for the common good. Public authorities, in this case, have the right and duty to impose on citizens the obligations necessary for national defense.[100]

The spiritual and moral fitness of the individual trooper, the unit, and even of the national command authority is an essential element in a nation's preparedness for and conduct of a just war. Military chaplains with the armies of modern Western nations are, in a sense, the conscience of commanders and troops, as well as leaders in prayer and worship among willing participants. Although the presence of good chaplains with combat soldiers greatly enhances unit morale, the main duties of chaplains are to strengthen the troops' relationship to God by bringing God's graces and mercies to those they serve and to advise commanders on the moral implications of their battlefield decisions. Ethical military decision making requires the application of both prudence and justice, and often goes well beyond legal requirements. The Geneva conventions and the Rules of Land Warfare reflect

---

[100] *Catechism of the Catholic Church*, nos. 2308–2310.

modern-day refinements in the application of moral principles during times of war, as the Code of Chivalry did in the early medieval era. In the long history of Christian soldiering in America and in Western nations, these conventions and rules help articulate a code of conduct for those engaged in a just war. *Pro Deo et patria* ("for God and country") should be the motto of all nations seeking justice and peace.

"The military world, now as in the past, often appears as a vehicle of evangelization and a privileged place for reaching the heights of holiness. I am thinking of the centurions of the Gospel; I am thinking of the first martyred soldiers and all throughout history who, by serving their sovereign land, learned how to become soldiers and witnesses of the one Lord Jesus Christ."[101] "Nor can I fail to mention the many soldiers engaged in the delicate work of resolving conflicts and restoring the necessary conditions for peace. I wish to remind them of the words of the Second Vatican Council: 'All those who enter the military in service to their country should look upon themselves as guardians of the security and freedom of their fellow countrymen; and in carrying out this duty properly, they too contribute to the establishment of peace.'"[102]

"Military service is a vocation, not simply a profession. In Christian belief, God created each of us for a purpose. He calls each of us by name to some form of service. No higher purpose exists than protecting other people, especially the weak and defenseless. This is why the Church, despite her historic resistance

---

[101] Pope John Paul II, address to military personnel during the *Anno Domini* 2000 Jubilee.
[102] Pope Benedict XVI, World Day of Peace message, January 1, 2006.

to war and armed violence, has held for many centuries that military service, when lived with a spirit of integrity, restraint, and justice, is virtuous. It is ennobling because, at its best, military service expresses the greatest of all virtues—charity, a sacrificial love for people and things outside and more important than oneself. It flows from something unique in the human heart—a willingness to place oneself in harm's way for the sake of others. The Church needs men and women of courage and Godliness today more than at any time in her history. So does this extraordinary country we call home in this world, a nation that still has an immense reservoir of virtue, decency, and people of good will. This is why the Catholic ideal of knighthood, with its demands of radical discipleship, is still alive and still needed. The essence of Christian knighthood remains the same—sacrificial service rooted in a living Catholic Faith. We serve our nation best by serving God first and by proving our faith with the example of our lives."[103]

"As we continue to probe into the actions of Saint Joan and their motives, we shall discover in her more and more the virtues that make a saint: faith, hope, and charity; and the same investigations will convince us that, unworldly as they are, these virtues inspired her life and alone can explain it. These three supreme virtues of a saint—faith, hope, and love of God—are bound to influence conduct deeply and to manifest themselves by the possession of natural virtues as well."[104]

---

[103] Archbishop Charles Chaput, talk at the United States Air Force Academy, October 2010.
[104] Robo, *Saint Joan: The Woman and the Saint*, 70, 79.

IV

The Invincible Prisoner

> *I thank you, Father, Lord of heaven and earth, that what you have hidden from the learned and the clever, you have revealed to the merest children. . . . When they take you before synagogues and before rulers and authorities, do not worry about how or what your defense will be or about what you are to say. For the Holy Spirit will teach you at that moment what you should say.*
>
> —Luke 10:21; 12:11–12 (NAB)

⚜

The Noble Captive

The twilight of the virgin soldier quickly became the dark night of her captivity. The Maid's "year of action" was over. Her "year of passion" had just begun. The Bastard of Wandomme, Count de Ligny of Luxembourg, and Duke Philip of Burgundy were exultant over the capture of the Maid. They had hit the monetary jackpot with their ransom trophy. The Duke of Bedford would pay them a fortune, a king's ransom, for their very valuable captive. "The Duke of Burgundy dashed off a letter to all the cities of the realm, as well as letters to rulers in other countries, thanking God for the capture of 'the woman they call the Maid,' a capture, he asserted, 'that would show the error and mad belief of all those who were in sympathy with the actions of this woman.'"[105] The Maid had been the nemesis of the English, humiliating them on battlefields, capturing their top commanders, and inspiring their opponents to rally themselves in combat at Orléans and Patay. Her capture was now the key for England to break the morale of Charles VII's French loyalists and their armies.

---

[105] Ó'Floinn, *Three French Saints: The One Who Led an Army*, 73.

Since she had surrendered to a knight of the enemy, Joan expected and received the basic chivalric courtesies associated with someone of her stature, at least for the period she was held by Duke John of Luxembourg. He permitted her brother Pierre and her squire, John d'Aulon, to stay with her during the first few months, while he paraded his captive Maid through much of the English and Burgundian occupied territory of France, both to demonstrate their superior military strength and to demoralize French sympathizers. Under armed escort they remained for a few days in the duke's camp, a short while at the town of Noyon, where the duke of Burgundy and his wife were residing, and then to the castle at Beaulieu, about thirty kilometers from Compiègne. Very soon after arriving at the castle, Joan made her first attempt to escape, after locking her guard in the room of her confinement; but the gatekeeper discovered her and brought her back to her quarters.

Beaurevoir

In early August the duke brought her to Beaurevoir, where his wife, Jeanne of Luxembourg, and his elderly aunt, Jeanne of Bethune, were residing. Both ladies were pious and most charitable toward Joan. They made her feel like a guest rather than a prisoner, offering her their fine women's clothes to wear while in their domicile. Joan politely declined the offer of female clothes, but accepted their gracious hospitality in other matters, such as religious devotions. By contrast, Haimond de Macy, a Burgundian knight who was a friend and frequent visitor at Beaurevoir, was physically attracted to Joan. On one occasion he brazenly tried to fondle her breasts, but was angrily rebuffed by the chaste virgin.[106] Lust in the heart and sexual aggression by many of

---

[106] Stolpe, *The Maid of Orléans*, 191–192.

her male captors and guards were to be constant threats to her. Consequently, while in captivity, as she had done with her own soldiers, Joan always prudently wore her male garb, both to reflect her modesty and to protect her virginal chastity.

Acting on the normal impulse of a captive soldier, Joan made another attempt to escape. Her place of confinement, however, was a room in a castle tower about twenty meters above ground; thus, any attempt to jump out was extremely dangerous and possibly fatal. Her concern, though, for the besieged citizens of Compiègne was so strong that she imprudently ignored the warning of her Voices not to jump. She managed to hang on to the ledge with her feet hanging down, before releasing her grip and falling to the ground. She lay stunned and unconscious for a long while. Then she awoke, although still badly bruised, and hid in the tower base for three days without food or water. All was for naught once a castle guard discovered her hideout and brought her back inside to a more secure area.

The aunt and the wife of the Duke of Luxembourg were both so kindly disposed toward the Maid that they urged the duke not to sell Joan to the Duke of Burgundy or to the Duke of Bedford. Sadly for Joan, the elderly and frail Jeanne of Bethune died, leaving the Maid without an important protector. Having secured the inheritance from his aunt, the Duke of Luxembourg then enhanced his wealth by auctioning the Maid to the highest bidder. All the while, her own people, French churchmen and noblemen alike, abandoned the Maid to the Burgundians and the English. Archbishop de Chartres declared that Joan was captured because of her pride, vainglory, and indulgence in fine clothing. Her own king, Charles VII, manipulated as he was also by his pro-Burgundy adviser Tremoille, made no earnest offer of ransom for her release. "No words can adequately describe the disgraceful ingratitude and apathy of Charles and his advisers in leaving the Maid to her fate. If military force had not availed, they had prisoners like the Earl of Suffolk in their hands, for which she could have been exchanged. Joan was sold by John of Luxembourg to the English for a sum which would amount to several hundred thousand dollars in modern money."[107]

The Anglo-Burgundian lawyers and theologians of the University of Paris, eager to ingratiate themselves with the English regent, had written the Duke of Burgundy only three days after the Maid's capture, asking that he send her to them for trial as a heretic. Yet those anti-French clerics could not possibly have matched the huge sum of money that Bedford himself, through his negotiator, Bishop Pierre Cauchon, eventually paid to the Dukes of Burgundy and Luxembourg to obtain their female nemesis. Perhaps Duke John of Luxembourg's guilty conscience caused him, on Saint Nicholas Day in early December 1430, to word his signed receipt of money for his sale of the valuable captive accurately as "Jeanne, who is called the Maid, a prisoner of war."[108] What an expensive gift the Regent Bedford had obtained for his nephew, the little boy king of England!

Rouen: The Prison Cell

In late December, Joan was moved to the English stronghold of Rouen, to a prison in the castle of the Earl of Warwick, a vassal of the Duke of Bedford. There she endured severe deprivation, humiliation, and threatened torture at the hands of English soldiers. Bedford wanted a Church tribunal to condemn Joan for witchcraft, prostitution, or heresy, since he and his English

---

[107] Thurston, *Catholic Encyclopedia*, s.v. "Joan of Arc."
[108] Ó'Floinn, *Three French Saints: The One Who Led an Army*, 79.

THE INVINCIBLE PRISONER

soldiers attributed her previous battlefield successes to demonic powers. He found his ideal chief judge in Pierre Cauchon, the very same person who had negotiated his purchase of the Maid from the Duke of Luxembourg.

Cauchon was the bishop of Beauvais who had been displaced from his diocese once that territory came under French control. That aristocratic bishop was also a strong supporter of the Duke of Burgundy along with the English regent. As a clever "theologian" and former rector at the University of Paris, he was the principal architect of the "dual monarchy" theory whereby Henry V's heir could become king of England and France. He also solicited endorsements from his colleagues at the university in order to be named presiding judge at the trial of the Maid. He obtained this role illicitly, since he was neither the bishop of the place where the Maid's alleged heresy occurred nor the bishop of her home diocese, as canon law then specified. But because Bedford wanted the Maid tried in Rouen under his control and where the archbishopric see was vacant, he and Cauchon pressured the priest-canons of that archdiocese to grant Cauchon a "commission of territory," authorizing the bishop of Beauvais to preside at the trial in their city. By conducting a "beautiful trial" according to all ecclesiastical and civil norms—and Bedford's pleasure—the ambitious and avaricious Cauchon saw an opportunity afterward to enhance his prestige and his benefices by gaining the archdiocese of Rouen for himself.

During the pretrial investigation, Cauchon sent his emissaries to Domrémy, hoping to find out something scandalous about the Maid to use against her. They returned to Rouen, however, only with many positive testimonials from the townsfolk, all highly commending Jeannette's virtuous character and charitable deeds. Yet the bishop included none of their statements in the official record. The bishop of Avranches wrote Cauchon a formal letter of protest against the illegality of the trial, a documented objection purposely omitted by Cauchon from the public records. Several Dominican theologians from Rouen also expressed their concern or total opposition, one of whom was even imprisoned by the unscrupulous bishop.[109]

The Trial

With Joan in her prison cell, Cauchon began his show trial with a ludicrous demand. Bedford and Cauchon, fully aware that Joan had made at least two previous escape and evasion attempts at other locations, ordered the English soldiers guarding her to chain her hands and feet to the wall of her dank dungeon cell, with three of them staying inside her cell and two others posted outside. Cauchon told Joan at the start of the trial to swear an oath that she would not try to escape "under penalty of being convicted of heresy." The holy Maid immediately rejected that crass intimidation by boldly declaring: "I do not accept that condition. If I did escape, how could that cause me to be blamed for having offended against my faith?"[110] Excepting supernatural intervention, the Maid had no real possibility of escape anyway. The Burgundian bishop presiding at the Church tribunal for the French prisoner of war in an English dungeon had only just begun to plumb the depths of obfuscation and deceit.

From the end of February to the end of March 1431, there were six preliminary examinations in the courtroom and nine more in the prison. Then in April the "fine trial" began, with the bishop of Beauvais presiding at the formal process—of

---

[109] Ó'Floinn, *Three French Saints: The One Who Led an Army*, 84.
[110] Ibid., 85.

condemnation. Yes, the predetermined verdict was condemnation of the Maid of Orléans. The English cardinal Henry Beaufort, uncle of the regent, Duke Bedford, co-presided with the Burgundian bishop. Cauchon selected a jury of judges who were favorable to his desired outcome, accomplishing this aim by threatening with imprisonment or torture any potential jurors who favored the French cause or who were kindly disposed toward their Maid. He "had assembled one cardinal, six bishops, thirty-two doctors of theology, sixteen bachelors of theology, seven doctors of medicine, and one hundred other clerical associates."[111]

Then he conducted the trial according to his prejudiced interpretation of canon law and civil law. In this he gave at least an initial appearance of lawfulness, seeming to abide by the letter of the law while ignoring other more important aspects of jurisprudence. Cauchon did not act at all according to the spirit of the law, which required an honest search for truth and justice, guilt or innocence. The bishop, of course, had to maintain the pretense of convening a Church trial to judge a supposed heretic or witch. He had to cloak the fact that this Maid was a prisoner of war and also a political prisoner, shackled in chains within a cell guarded by English men, rather than in a Church prison guarded by religious women.

"Therefore before us, your competent judges, namely Pierre, by divine mercy bishop of Beauvais, and brother Jean Le Maistre, vicar in this city and diocese of the notable master Jean Graverent, Inquisitor of Heretical Error in the kingdom of France, and especially appointed by him to officiate in this cause: you, Jeanne, commonly called The Maid, have been

---

[111] Mary Gordon, *Joan of Arc* (New York: Penguin, 2000), 105.

arraigned to account for many pernicious crimes and have been charged in a matter of the Faith."[112] Cauchon assigned three professional notaries to record the proceedings in French, whose transcripts would later be translated into Latin for the official Church records. As the trial proceeded and Joan's inspired responses began to embarrass her chief judge, he ordered that her answers be loosely rendered rather than verbatim. He also tried to make her swear another oath to tell all about everything they asked. She refused, of course, saying she was already sworn to secrecy by her Voices about certain matters not relevant to their inquiries.

The judges proceeded with a line of interrogation to discredit the Maid's Voices.

"Does the Archangel wear clothes?" they asked.

"Do you not think God has the power to clothe him?" she quipped.

"What were your saints wearing?" they persisted.

Without being too specific, she answered: "God clothes each in splendor with a crown on her head."

"What about that 'fairy tree'? Did you sing and dance around it? Is that where you saw and heard your voices?" With that type of questioning they tried to associate her with superstition or witchcraft or even orgies. To the contrary, she referred to the tree in the Bois Chenu ("ancient woods") as the "Lady Tree" where she occasionally sang but did not dance, then gathered flowers to bring to the shrine of Our Lady of Bermont on her Saturday visits. She also testified that in her earlier youth, her saints spoke or appeared to her only near the Domrémy church.

---

[112] *The Trial of Jeanne D'Arc*, the official Latin record, trans. William P. Barrett (New York: Gotham House, 1932), 364.

Questions also arose regarding Church authority versus individual conscience, public revelation versus private, and the dogmatic versus the mystical. The casuists among the expert theologians and clerics claimed supreme authority as the Church Militant (the visible Church on earth), as the sole arbiters of the public revelation of God in Christ. Hence, from their narrow perspective, Joan's references to Christ with His angels and saints triumphant in heaven—according to her interior, private revelations as a simple, illiterate, female layperson—demonstrated her disobedience and disrespect for the Church of God vested in them as highly credentialed clergymen. In reality, the prayerful, humble Maid had insight into the Church Triumphant (the members of the Church in heaven). Her judges were blinded by their own pride and arrogance, in attempting to trap her into separating herself from the Church by rejecting their usurped authority.

After an old archdeacon named John de Chatillon explained the nature of the term to her, Joan replied: "I do believe in the Church on earth, but, as I have already declared, as far as what I have done and said are concerned, I trust in God and refer myself to Him. I believe that the Church Militant cannot err or fail, but I submit all my words and deeds to God, Who caused me to do what I have done."[113] Joan made no intellectual separation between the Church Militant, the Church Triumphant, and the Church Suffering (the souls in purgatory). Her beautiful, mystical response, certainly inspired by the Holy Spirit, was: "But why do you try to confuse me? Christ's Church is all one and the same!"

[113] John Beevers, *Saint Joan of Arc* (Rockford, IL: TAN Books, 1974), 153.

Chatillon then revisited the subject of her male attire, which he considered to be indecent, scandalous, and immoral on her part. In his opinion, she who was a woman in the guise of a man acted contrary to the commandments of God, the virtue of modesty, and acceptable social standards. Joan countered that insinuation of immorality by referring the trial judges to the Church tribunal record of 1429 at Poitiers, where she had answered all questions regarding her faith and morals and won the strong endorsement of those French Church officials and thus of Charles VII.

In fact, the well-known and highly esteemed theologian John Gerson, ousted from the University of Paris because of his loyalty to France, had written very favorably about La Pucelle. Regarding male clothing on a woman or even female clothing on a man, he noted from the Holy Scriptures and from history that some circumstances of modesty or secrecy could warrant the cross-dressing. Regarding the spiritual life, he also commented that the individual soul could receive messages and visions from God or His saints and angels, and that a person's conscience must be respected.

Cauchon admitted none of the previous Church investigations or any favorable opinions about the Maid into his process of condemnation. He had only contempt for Joan's conscience.

Her interrogators saw in Joan's refusal to don women's clothing the opportunity to charge her with immorality and disobedience to Church authority in order to justify their guilty verdict and condemn her to death. No other charges against her could be substantiated, so they spent much time pressing her on that issue. At one session in court, after being questioned yet again on the subject of male clothes, Joan suddenly ignored the trial judges and began praying: "Very sweet God, in honor of Your

Holy Passion, I beg You, if You love me, that You reveal to me how I should answer these men of the church. I know well, regarding my clothes, the command that I received; but I do not know anything about the manner in which I should drop it. On that, may it please You to instruct me."[114]

The long and tedious interrogations by numerous judges, several of them shouting questions at Joan, fatigued not only their prisoner but also the judges themselves. One of them, tired also of the obvious injustice against the Maid, was Master John Lohier. After reading all the documents in her case, he refused to take part in the court process, declaring "They ought not to proceed against Joan in the matter of faith."[115] Nevertheless, Cauchon continued with his show trial. In a ploy not in accord with juridical procedures, he ordered her to recite the Lord's Prayer. Again Joan retorted with a challenge to him: "I will recite that prayer for you if you hear my confession."[116] She knew that any matters of her faith or morals revealed to him in the confessional would clear her of any hint of heresy and that the bishop would be bound in conscience by the seal of confession to absolve her of any guilt and then to dismiss the charges against her of heresy and immorality. Of course, the wily and unscrupulous bishop did not accept her challenge. After numerous repeated questions posed by "the learned and the clever" clerics, one after the other badgering her, she exclaimed, "If it were not for the grace of God, I would not know how to do anything!"

There immediately followed a trick question posed by one of her harshest judges: "Do you know that you are in the grace of

---

[114] Pernoud and Clin, *Joan of Arc: Her Story*, 121.
[115] Robo, *Saint Joan: The Woman and the Saint*, 132.
[116] Ó'Floinn, *Three French Saints: The One Who Led an Army*, 85.

God?" Joan's inspired response to him was: "If I am not in the state of grace, may God put me there; if I am, may He keep me there!"[117] The shrewd judge wanted her to say with presumption that she was certain to be in the state of grace, so that the court could trap her in the sin of pride, in an arrogant reliance on herself. Or if their prisoner said that she was not in the state of grace, they could therefore conclude that her soul was in the state of mortal sin, under the influence of the Devil, and thus not truly sent on a mission from Almighty God. The trial notary recorded her words verbatim and testified years later that "those who were interrogating her were all astonished." And so also were theologians throughout Europe amazed by her remarks, once the trial transcripts had been widely circulated.[118]

Her verbal testimony was summarized with her response to the ultimate question whether she loved the Lord, Almighty God: "I love God with all my heart. I trust Him completely with my whole life. My works and my deeds are all in the hand of God, and I refer to Him. And I assure you that I would want to do or say nothing that is against the Christian Faith."[119] She did not presume to judge herself, but left that judgment to Christ, the most trustworthy and just Judge.

During her trial, Joan had no advocate for her defense, only prosecutorial harassment and villainy from Burgundian churchmen. The official prosecutor was John d'Estivet, a priest of Cauchon's own diocese of Beauvais, who, like his bishop, was a fugitive from that French-controlled city, a hater of the Maid and King Charles, and also very ambitious for monetary benefits

---

[117] Ó'Floinn, *Three French Saints: The One Who Led an Army*, 86.
[118] Ibid., 87.
[119] Tavard, *The Spiritual Way of St. Jeanne d'Arc*, 69.

from the English. Estivet was furthermore a foul-mouthed, lewd detractor of Joan whose contempt for her evidenced itself in his public harangues in the courtroom and his private slurs in her prison cell. The two of them trumped up charges of witchcraft, heresy, and prostitution against her; and finally tried to trap her with theological nuances, doctrinal ploys, and other subterfuges. Cauchon even sent another one of his lackeys, the priest Nicholas Loiseleur, pretending to be from Joan's home region of Lorraine, to win her trust, hear her confession (with Cauchon listening from outside), and obtain knowledge of her confessed sins for use against her in court. They both sacrilegiously disregarded their sacred orders forbidding any revelation of sins confessed to them in the sacrament of Penance, a very serious sin warranting their own immediate excommunication from the Church!

In mid-April Joan was given a piece of rotten fish sent to her by Cauchon, which she unwittingly ate. She became extremely sick, thinking herself about to die. Cauchon and Bedford, fearing her death might upset their shrewd legal plan for her demise, immediately sent for medical assistance. One of the doctors made a thorough examination of his important patient, also noting once again that Joan was truly an intact virgin. He reportedly used leeches to bleed her and other medicinal means to relieve the excruciating abdominal pains, thereby prolonging her life temporarily. Despite the doctors' best efforts to rehabilitate her, Joan continued to suffer weakness and ill health from the food poisoning as from the harsh, cruel circumstances of being chained to the wall in a cold cell, harassed by foul male guards who would not let her sleep and even tried to violate her virginity. To add insult to injury, Estivet, the maniacal priest-prosecutor, repeatedly called Joan "a slut and a whore, offering her many other insults," as the doctors of medicine themselves later testified.[120]

The devious clergy among her trial judges surprised Joan with the question of two popes, which had already been resolved by the year 1415. Unaware of the persistent political effects of the previous Western Church schism but nonetheless inspired by the Holy Spirit, the unschooled teenager appealed for judgment of her case to the "pope in Rome," as had been suggested by a sympathetic cleric, Friar Isambert. The enraged Cauchon immediately shouted at him: "Hold your tongue, in the Devil's name!" That unscrupulous bishop, a willing pawn of the English regent, straightaway rejected Joan's canonical right of appeal, since he intended to trap and convict her of heresy, apostasy, witchcraft, and disobedience to the "Church Militant," then to have her turned over to "the secular arm" (the English) to be burned to death. Their lip service to the pope belied their traitorous politics. Cauchon and his cabal had signed, sealed, and delivered the Maid to their English overlord Bedford.

As Cauchon wrapped up his "fine, beautiful trial," he consulted the other judges for their input. But, despite the many weeks of courtroom interrogations, he and his prosecutor had not convinced a majority of them to vote the Maid guilty of sinning against the Faith. They considered life in prison rather than death to be a just sentence. Ignoring them all, Cauchon proceeded with his verdict and sentence in order to please Bedford. The English boy king's secretary, John Rinel, acting on orders from the regent Bedford, threatened to take Joan to an English civil court if Cauchon's ecclesiastical judges rendered anything other than a verdict of condemnation.

---

[120] Ó'Floinn, *Three French Saints: The One Who Led an Army*, 91.

THE INVINCIBLE PRISONER

After her trial, the presiding judge further disgraced himself by making several attempts to alter the official written transcripts from Joan's actual spoken words. Rebuffing Cauchon, however, one of the principal trial clerks, the cleric Manchon, courageously refused to suborn his oath of office by falsifying her documented testimony as Cauchon had demanded. Cauchon also solicited theological opinions of professors from the University of Paris. All of those "learned" theologians had solidly pro-English, pro-Burgundian dispositions and thus were rabidly hostile toward the Maid and King Charles, whom she supported. Besides, none of them was actually present during the trial proceedings, nor had any of them even seen or questioned the Maid. Nevertheless, Cauchon included their prejudiced opinions in the court record.

The time came for Joan to hear the decision of the court. As she listened to the seventy-two articles of indictment read to her by Estivet, she protested vigorously against the distortions and lies contained in them. Her angry retort to the falsehood about her male clothes being very short and dissolute was omitted from the official Latin translation, although it remained in the original, notarized French text. Cauchon had Estivet shorten the long list of supposed offenses to twelve articles of indictment and conviction, including the cross-dressing issue and Joan's rejection of their "Church Militant" position.

In mid-May the Rouen sheriff's deputy, John Massieu, who was Joan's usher from cell to courtroom and back, brought her to the great tower of the castle. There Cauchon himself with two assessors and the executioner with his assistant met her. After seeing the instruments of torture and being threatened with their use on her, Joan still resisted: "You can pull all my body apart if you wish until my soul leaves my body, but I will not tell you anything else; and if I did tell you something, afterwards I shall say it was only because you made me say it by torture."[121] They decided against the torture treatment for expediency, thinking that by it their prisoner still would not yield to them and that they would surely be censured for having ordered it over the objections of a majority of the trial assessors.

The Saint-Ouen Cemetery

Early in the morning of May 24, dressed in a female penitent's clothes and with her head shaved, Joan was taken in a cart by a large contingent of English soldiers to the cemetery of the Abbey of Saint-Ouen. That was the first time in a couple of months that she had been outside in the open air and sunlight. A large crowd of civilians had assembled with the soldiers, expecting a quick ceremony by the clergy, then a transfer of the Maid to the secular authorities for execution, if she did not abjure her prior testimony. "There were three platforms: one for Cauchon and the tribunal, a second for the bishops and clergy from Rouen and its environs, and the third for Beaufort, the cardinal of England. There was a high scaffold on which Joan and the preacher would be visible to the crowd. The condensed indictment of twelve articles was read aloud. Then the preacher gave a pious sermon. William Erard, a priest of the Rouen cathedral, spoke on a scriptural text 'a tree does not bear fruit of itself.'"[122] The rules of the Inquisition required a pious admonition with a call to repentance; but his sermon was really a vicious diatribe against the Maid. She silently endured insult after insult. Then Erard started berating and disparaging her king, calling him a heretic and a schismatic. Joan vigorously interrupted him: "Condemn

---

[121] Ó'Floinn, *Three French Saints: The One Who Led an Army*, 95.
[122] Cf. Gordon, *Joan of Arc*, 125–126.

THE INVINCIBLE PRISONER

me, if you will, but not the king! By my faith, sir, with all respect, I say and swear to you, on pain of my life, that he is the most noble Christian of all; and no one loves the faith and the Church better than he; and he is not at all what you say!" Erard turned to Massieu and said, "Make her be quiet!"[123]

"Regarding all my words and deeds, I appeal first of all to God. I also wish the record to be sent to Rome and put before the pope, for everything I did was at God's command!" Once again they told her that the pope was too far away and that the bishop of the diocese had complete jurisdiction over her. Three times Erard read his assertions and then ordered Joan to sign her submission. She was presented with a parchment having about eight lines of text on it. Her usher, Massieu, read the short text aloud to Joan, in the hearing of the officials and some in the crowd of onlookers. It supposedly indicated her renunciation of errors against faith and morals and an abjuration of her prior testimony, her submission to Church authority, and her agreement to wear female garb. Cauchon and his company of churchmen promised "compassion" if she signed it: they would reduce her sentence to life in a Church prison guarded by females, with permission to receive the sacraments. "Sign it now or you will end your life by fire!" insisted Erard.

The physical strain of her recent illness, compounded by five months of harsh imprisonment, had obviously taken its toll also on her mental and emotional state. She signed the document with a circle rather than in her own name *Jehanne*, which she had learned to do by then; but Calot, the cardinal's secretary, forced her hand to inscribe a cross on the parchment.

---

[123] Frances Gies, *Joan of Arc, the Legend and the Reality* (New York: Harper and Row, 1981), 212.

To the Englishman the cross indicated a true confession; but to the French, as Joan intended, it secretly meant that the words preceding it were not to be believed! Two of the priests heard Joan utter a strange laugh as she apparently abjured her prior testimony. A number of those present later remarked that Joan seemed not to know what she was doing by signing the parchment; but under duress, she signed it nonetheless.

Then a commotion broke out among the English gentry and their soldiers because the "Church Militant" had agreed to reduce the Maid's sentence to life in prison. Bedford was furious with Cauchon and upset with his uncle the cardinal for allowing that outcome. They thought Cauchon had let "the bird out of the cage, that the king's money had been wasted," as also Warwick angrily expressed the English dismay. Some of the English soldiers even threw stones at the Burgundian clergy, while others brandished their swords to threaten the returning judges and assessors. In their testiness, the Burgundian bishop and the English cardinal's own secretary hurled insults at each other. "Come now, you churchmen; take me to your prisons and I will no longer be in the hands of the English," Joan said to Massieu and the prosecutor Estivet. When they asked Cauchon about it, he said, "Take her back where she came from."[124]

Meanwhile, Warwick's complaints to Cauchon about the waste of their king's money got a rapid response from one of the bishop's close collaborators, "My lord, do not worry; we shall soon catch her again." The English needed patience for a little while longer to get their money's worth from Cauchon and company. But the impatient soldiers, wanting to see the French "witch" burn that same day, only intensified their insults, not just

---

[124] Gies, *Joan of Arc, the Legend and the Reality*, 215.

to the clergy but especially toward the Maid as she was being led back to the castle dungeon—the same dreaded English prison cell. Joan's anxieties increased dramatically, once she realized she had been duped by the deceitful bishop. Just one day in the dark dungeon surrounded by crass enemy soldiers was torture for her; more time than that was like living in hell.

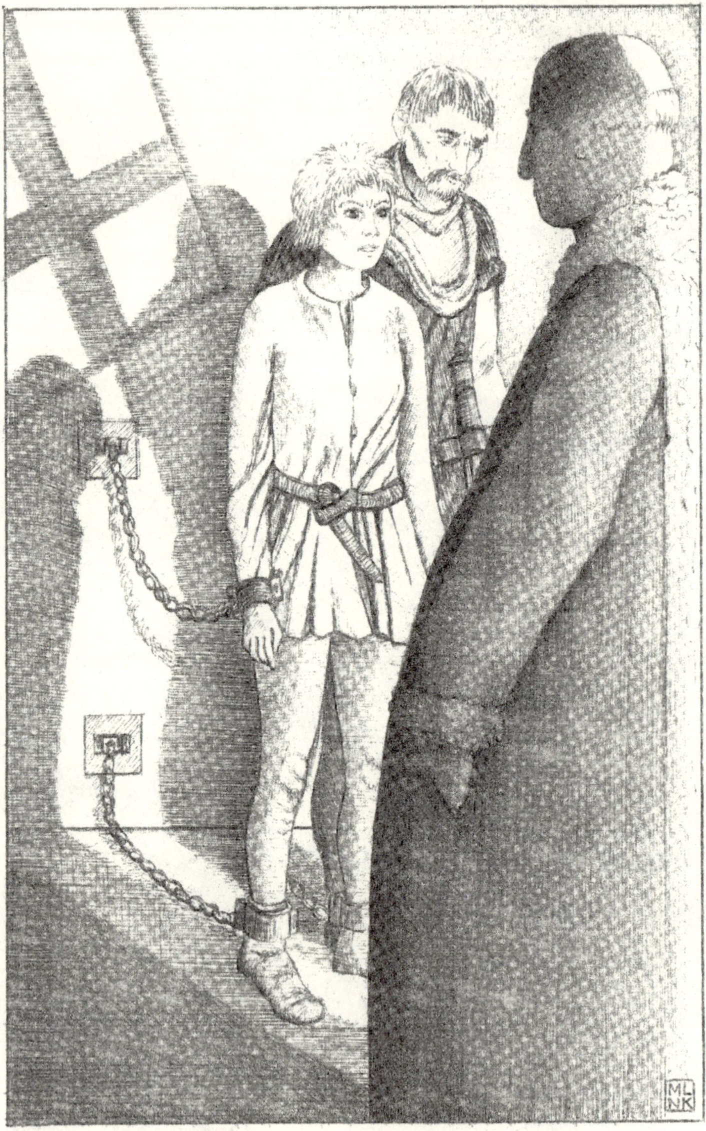

THE INVINCIBLE PRISONER

✤ Meditation ✤

THE PERSECUTED PATRIOT

"For this I was born and for this I came into the world, to testify to the truth. Everyone who belongs to the truth listens to my voice" (John 18:37). These words spoken by Jesus Christ, while being cynically interrogated by the Gentile Roman governor Pontius Pilate, could also be attributed to Joan the Maid. She was a political prisoner of the English, their prisoner of war, harshly guarded and mocked by crude male soldiers. Yet she had been on trial in a "French" Church court, whose sanctimonious judges did not render her any basic human decency and refused to recognize both the truth and dignity of her Christian womanhood and her mission from God. Jehanne d'Arc was born onto the world scene for the very same reason as Christ Jesus, the same reason also why every human person is conceived and born: to testify to the truth. Almighty God creates men and women in the divine image as distinct persons; and then, by their freely willed faith, God the Holy Spirit in Christ reconciles sinners and transforms them into virtuous, holy persons—into saints, who are beautiful images of the Divine Beauty.

The passion of Jeanne La Pucelle became like the Passion of Jesus the Christ: betrayal, trial, suffering, and death for the sins of the people. Jesus was an innocent man condemned in place of a guilty nation that had lost its reference to God. Caiaphas, the leading high priest of the Jewish religious court, the Sanhedrin, condemned Jesus for blasphemy. In an abuse of his religious oath, he used political expediency to send Jesus to Pilate: "[I]t is better for you that one man should die instead of the people" (John 11:50). Not just Israelites and Romans, but the peoples of

England and France too, along with many Catholic clergymen, had lost their honor by not upholding true faith in God and basic moral principles of personal integrity and social justice. The English moreover, because of their superstitious fear of the French Maid and their shame about the dread she produced in their soldiers, determined at all costs to take her life. They could not legitimately execute her for defeating them in battle; but they could coax a willing Burgundian bishop to sentence Joan the Maid to death as a witch and a heretic.

The training of every soldier in any army always includes not just the use of battle gear and weaponry, tactics and discipline, but also his responsible actions in the event of capture by the enemy. Escape, evasion, and survival in hostile territory while seeking to rejoin friendly forces are all part of the training, especially in modern armies. In the United States Army, a loyal soldier, if captured by enemy forces, must reveal to his captors only name, rank, and service number, despite torture and threat of death if he does not divulge his unit battle formations and future plans and operations. Many other armies and hostile combatants in these modern times, however, have no reference to true faith in God or to the natural moral law; they disregard the Geneva conventions and the Rules of Land Warfare, which require humane treatment of prisoners of war and noncombatant detainees. Moreover, some modern-day combatants consider even self-destruction as a weapon of war and consider suicide rather than capture to be an honorable option.

Although Joan of Arc had not trained for battle in any conventional way in late medieval times, she instinctively knew that an imprisoned soldier loyal to his country would make every possible attempt to break away from enemy captivity. Yes, she was surely imprudent and perhaps rash in her earlier and very

THE INVINCIBLE PRISONER

dangerous escape attempt from the Beaurevoir tower; but she was not suicidal; rather, she was most anxious to return to the battlefield to complete her mission from God to expel the English from her France. That zeal for God and country still exists in many of our nobler and more heroic soldiers, both those who have endured long years as prisoners of war and those who have been immobilized or incapacitated by combat injuries, longing to return to their comrades-in-arms.

"For the Holy Spirit will teach you at that moment what you should say" (Luke 12:12). That promise of Jesus to His disciples certainly held true in the case of Joan of Arc, especially in her responses to the deceitful bishop Cauchon and his iniquitous inquisitors. In her rebuttals to their continuous and vicious slanders, Joan always displayed virtuousness, especially divine wisdom to expose their foolishness and holy fortitude to deflect their malice, "flaming arrows of the evil one" (Eph. 6:16). Her resolute will, in the face of torture and humiliation, to do the holy will of God testified to her faithful love for God and for His Church, despite the hypocrisy and corruption of so many churchmen. And she demonstrated her loyalty and faithful love for her country, despite the indifference and cowardice by so many of her own countrymen and her king.

Joan's life as a brave and bold leader of the French army has brought her a certain historical fame, both in the eyewitness accounts of her contemporaries and in thousands of accounts down to our own time, six centuries later. Yet her year as a prisoner of war reveals an even more important dimension of her character in testifying to the truth of her mission from God. Her relationship with God was first and foremost in her heart and soul, even when her interrogators attempted to confuse her by separating her love into compartments—that is, to trap her into saying she loved God but not the Church, which they were supposed to be representing. In her long imprisonment, Joan endured the full wrath of the English as their prisoner of war and also their political prisoner. But the perfidy of Burgundian clergymen surely intensified the spiritual evils assaulting the holy Maid. All of her opponents were guilty of malice in one form of vice or another. Their lies and lusts, their avarice and cowardice served only to condemn them, her opponents, rather than impugn the integrity of the truly just and innocent Maid. That ignominious, iniquitous trial in Rouen recalls very vividly the most sacrilegiously evil trial in all human history, that of the Lord Jesus Christ in Jerusalem in A.D. 33.

"The time of my departure is at hand," wrote Saint Paul to Saint Timothy. "I have kept the faith.... [T]he crown of righteousness awaits me, which the Lord, the just judge, will award to me on that day" (2 Tim. 4:6–8). "As we do battle and fight in the contest of faith, God, his Angels, and Christ himself watch us. How exalted is the glory, how great the joy of engaging in a contest with God presiding, of receiving a crown with Christ as Judge! Dear brethren, let us arm ourselves with all our might; let us prepare ourselves for the struggle by innocence of heart, integrity of faith, dedication to virtue," exclaimed Saint Cyprian, third-century bishop and martyr.

"See how many are my enemies, see how fiercely they hate me. Preserve my soul and rescue me; do not let me be disgraced, for in you I seek refuge. Let integrity and uprightness preserve me; I wait for you, O LORD" (Ps. 25:19–21).

V

The Heroic Martyr

Christ also suffered for you, leaving you an example that you should follow in his footsteps.

—1 Peter 2:21

Beloved, do not be surprised that a trial by fire is occurring among you. But rejoice to the extent that you share in the sufferings of Christ, so that when his glory is revealed you may also rejoice exultantly.

—1 Peter 4:12–13

⚜

The Trial Sequel

Back in the living hell of her prison cell, Joan, still dressed in female penitential clothing, endured further outrages by the incensed guards. But they were under strict orders not to harm her physically in any way. That prohibition, however, did not seem to apply to the "nobility." Several aristocrats among the English, Burgundians, and Luxembourgers, who had been enjoying a celebratory meal in Warwick's castle at which Beaufort, Cauchon, and some other bishops were also present, afterward went into Joan's cell to mock and deride her further.

The Duke of Luxembourg baited her with an offer of release, but Joan saw through his ruse: "You mock me, since you have neither the power nor the will to do that. Even if there were a hundred thousand *godons* [the French derisive term for the constantly cursing English soldiers], England will never keep the holy kingdom of France from the King of heaven, my sovereign Lord!"

Enraged by that remark, the earl of Stafford drew his dagger to kill her, but was restrained by Warwick.

Later that same night, one of those high-ranking English nobles returned to the dungeon, entered Joan's cell, and sexually assaulted and battered her in an attempted rape. Someone else also secretly brought men's clothes into her cell, and laid them next to her mat. Only God knows what other demonic attacks she endured.

Right after the vicious assault, Joan donned the male clothing at her feet. "I [Martin Ladvenu] heard it from her lips that a great English lord entered her prison and tried to take her by force. That was the cause, she said, of her resuming a man's clothes.... And in fact, I [Isambert de La Pierre] saw her tearful, her face covered with tears, disfigured and outraged in such sort that I had pity and compassion on her."[125]

Yet throughout the three or four more days of terror in the prison, the Lord God did send His saints both to correct and to console His daughter Joan.

When Cauchon heard she had resumed male clothing, he himself went to her cell on May 28. Bruised and disheveled, Joan complained bitterly to him for his breach of promise in returning her to the lustful, hateful, and violent Englishmen. The bishop evidently had no remorse for his actions: after all, he had sent her back there among her enemies in order to trap her into resuming male clothing. He himself had been in the castle dining room enjoying his wine and dinner the night of the debauchery in Joan's cell. He was probably the one who planned that special delivery of male clothes to her cell, so she would "relapse" into her former "immoral" attire in "disobedience" to the "Church

---

[125] Régine Pernoud, *Joan of Arc by Herself and Her Witnesses*, trans. Edward Hyams (New York: Stein and Day, 1966), 220.

Militant." A dialogue ensued as part of a mini trial, a short sequel to the completed formal process:

Question: Why have you assumed this male attire and who made you take it?

JOAN. I have taken it of my own will. I have taken it because it is more licit and fitting to have man's clothes since I am with men than to have women's clothes. I have assumed it because what had been promised me has not been observed, to wit that I should go to Mass and should receive the Body of Christ and should be taken out of irons.

PIERRE CAUCHON. Have you not made abjuration and promised especially not to resume man's clothes?

JOAN. I would rather die than remain in irons; but if it be permitted me to go to Mass and I be taken out of irons and that I be put in a gracious [Church] prison, and that I have women,[126] I will be good and do what the Church wishes.

CAUCHON. Since that Thursday, have you heard the voices of Saints Catherine and Margaret?

JOAN. Yes.

CAUCHON. What did they tell you?

JOAN. God has sent to me by Saints Catherine and Margaret great pity for the mighty betrayal to which I consented in making abjuration and revocation in order to save my life; and that I was damning myself to save my life. [Here the clerk noted in the margin, *"responsio mortifera,"* "a fatal answer."] If I said that God had not sent me, I should damn myself. It is true that God sent me. My Voices have since told me that I did a great injury

---

[126] "That I have women" appears only in the French text, not in the official Latin.

in confessing that I had not done well in what I had done. All that I said and revoked that Thursday, I did only because of fear of the fire.[127]

Cauchon then questioned Joan once again about the authenticity of her saints and about the mysterious crown that she or her angel placed on her king's head. Joan finalized her responses thus: "And all I have done I did for fear of the fire and I revoked nothing but [that which] was against the truth. I would rather make my penitence once and for all, that is to say die, than to suffer any longer the pain of being in prison. I have never done anything against God and against the faith, whatever I may have been made to revoke. And for what was contained in the *cedule* [her signed concession] of abjuration, I did not understand it. I did not mean to revoke anything unless provided it pleased God. If the judges wish it, I will resume woman's clothes; for the rest, I will do nothing about it."[128]

Finally Cauchon obtained his evidence that the Maid had relapsed into disobedience and immorality. "That heard, we went away from her to proceed thereafter according to law and reason."[129] Cardinal Beaufort with Bishop Cauchon called an assembly of forty-two of the assessors who had participated in the formal process, informing them of Joan's breach of her promise and relapse into her "errors" and asking for their opinions in sentencing her. Amazingly only three of them favored handing her over to the secular authorities for death. Yet the overwhelming majority of dissenting judges and assessors had merely a consulta-

---

[127] Régine Pernoud, *Joan of Arc by Herself and Her Witnesses*, 221–222.
[128] Ibid., 222, quoting the official record c. 395–399.
[129] Ibid.

tive voice in the matter, no actual decision-making authority of judgment by jury. Beaufort and Cauchon with their tiny minority of sycophants did what they had decided long before that day: they condemned Joan and turned her over to the "secular arm" of their English overlords.[130]

The Final Condemnation

The bishop of Beauvais wrapped up the sequel to his "fine trial" by issuing his final decision in the case. After the usual references to his holy office and authority "by divine mercy," he decreed to his priests and the people of Rouen on May 29:

> For certain causes and reasons more extensively set forth elsewhere, a certain woman, commonly called Jeanne the Maid, relapsed into many errors against the orthodox faith, after a public abjuration of those errors before the face of the Church, has fallen into them once more, as is and has been duly proven by her statements, assertions, and otherwise. Therefore, we expressly command and enjoin each one of you as he shall be required, without waiting for or excusing yourself because of another, to summon the said Jeanne to appear in person before Us at eight o'clock tomorrow morning in the Old Market Place of Rouen, in order to hear Us declare her relapsed, excommunicate, and heretic, with the intimation customary in such cases."[131]

Cauchon rambled on with his tedious legalese, justifying himself by presumptuously using the divine "We" or "Us" in the

---

[130] Cf. Ó'Floinn, *Three French Saints: The One Who Led an Army*, 99–100.
[131] Barrett, *The Trial of Jeanne D'Arc*, 358 359.

text, as if he were the pope and the Holy Spirit were speaking directly through him. Although he referred often to himself as "Pierre, bishop by divine mercy," he certainly had not shown Joan any mercy, divine or human. Moreover he lied in the transcript, suggesting he had the authority and approval of the pope in Rome and that the Maid had refused an appeal to the Holy See, whereas Cauchon had in fact rejected her appeal.

Then Cauchon addressed Joan directly:

> Therefore we declare that you are fallen again into your former errors; and under the sentence of excommunication which you originally incurred, we decree that you are a relapsed heretic; and by this sentence which we deliver in writing and pronounce from this tribunal, we denounce you as a rotten member, which, so that you shall not infect the other members of Christ, must be cast out of the unity of the Church, cut off from her Body, and given over to the secular power: we cast you off, separate and abandon you, praying this same secular power on this side of death and the mutilation of your limbs, to moderate its judgment toward you and, if true signs of repentance appear in you, to permit the sacrament of penance to be administered to you.[132]

Cauchon's crassly hypocritical, deceitful, and unjust conduct of the trial, with its foregone conclusion, showed itself throughout his final decree. The English-Burgundian case against Joan was closed even before it opened; the guilty verdict with sentence of condemnation and death came even before the trial started. In actual fact, the English had planned to burn the Maid as a

---

[132] Barrett, *The Trial of Jeanne D'Arc*, 362.

witch or a heretic once they captured her—or bought her from her captors. She exclaimed to Cauchon: "Bishop, I die through you! I appeal to God, the Great Judge, for the terrible evils and injustices done to me: for this I summon you before God!"[133]

Perhaps the Burgundian bishop had a slight qualm of conscience after Joan's stern admonishment of him and after her many appeals to receive the sacraments. In the morning of May 30, 1431, the day of her execution, Bishop Cauchon finally allowed Friar Martin Ladvenu to hear her confession, in which she renounced all resentment against her enemies, and to give her Holy Communion. That year, May 30 was also the eve of Corpus Christi, the annual solemn liturgical celebration of the Body of Christ in the Most Blessed Sacrament. But Cauchon ordered someone else to bring the Eucharist secretly, without candles and sacred ceremony, in order that his own very public condemnation of Joan as a relapsed heretic and apostate would not appear contradictory when permitting her the sacraments of Christ and the Church. Father Martin, however, chided the other priest and insisted that the Holy Eucharist of Christ be respected by using a white surplice over his cassock robe with a priestly stole and having the acolytes carry lighted candles and ring a bell during a proper procession to her cell. Once the procession had arrived, Ladvenu reverently fed Joan with the Bread of Life, her Viaticum, her Lord "on the way with" her. Jesus, the Divine Mercy, came at last to Joan!

The Stake

Then her usher led the Maid outdoors from her prison cell onto a cart pulled by a donkey to the place of execution in the old

---

[133] Robo, *Saint Joan: The Woman and the Saint*, 151.

marketplace near the Church of Saint-Sauveur (Holy Savior). "Heretic-Relapsed-Apostate-Idolatress," written on the dunce cap on Joan's head in mockery, identified the condemned and abandoned Maid. She was dressed in the coarse garb of a female penitent with her hair shaved close to her scalp, "accompanied by more than eight hundred men of war with axes and swords."[134] Joan's procession to the stake must have greatly resembled the sorrowful way of Jesus' carrying the Cross to Calvary. Observing her, the priest Loiseleur, who earlier in the trial had violated the seal of confession with Joan, was evidently so stung to the heart with remorse that he jumped into the cart with her to beg her forgiveness. In so doing, he was himself on the verge of being put to death by the furious English soldiers! Her enemies wanted Joan to be seen, not as the once glorious Maid of Orléans and an innocent martyr, but as a pathetic, disfigured outcast, rejected by Church and state.

Once on the platform at the stake, Joan heard another admonishing sermon. While Nicholas Midy harangued Joan in his "pious" polemic,

> she showed great constancy and very peaceably listened to the preaching of the final sermon, showing great sign and evidence and clear appearance of her contrition, penitence, and fervor of faith: as much by her pious and devout lamentations and invocations of the Blessed Trinity and of the blessed glorious Virgin Mary and of all the blessed saints of Paradise ... as in requesting also pardon most humbly of all manner of people of whatever condition and estate, whether of her own party or the other,

---

[134] Robo, *Saint Joan: The Woman and the Saint*, 151.

requesting that they would pray for her, and forgiving them the evil that they had done her. She persevered and continued for a very long space of time, as about a half an hour ... at which the judges there present and even several Englishmen were provoked to tears and to weeping, and indeed most bitterly wept at it.[135]

Such was the later testimony of her usher, Massieu.

The partisan clergy and aristocracy had a preferential viewing area for the execution by fire. Among them were Cardinal Beaufort; Bishop Cauchon with two other bishops and his vice-inquisitor, Lemaître; Louis of Luxembourg, who had sold Joan; several other ardent partisans of the English; and of course, the English regent, Duke John of Bedford, and his entourage. By contrast with the Maid's remarkable serenity of soul, the English and their supporters were very impatient to get the fire going and get rid of their nemesis. One of them said to a nearby cleric, "What? Priest, will you make us dine here?!"[136] Cauchon completely ignored the canonical requirement to render the condemned person to the local secular judges of that place — namely, to the sheriff and civic authorities of Rouen, who alone had legal responsibility to determine the sentence and any punishment due. Instead, the bishop of Beauvais issued his condemnation and then left the scene. Joan turned to the friars near her for comfort and then declared, "With God's help, I shall be with Him in paradise."[137] The English executioner, Geoffrey Therage, immediately grabbed Joan and led her to the stake.

---

[135] Pernoud, *Joan of Arc by Herself and Her Witnesses*, 229, quoting Quicherat's translation, 236–237.
[136] Ibid., 231.
[137] Spoto, *Joan: The Mysterious Life of the Heretic Turned Saint*, 185.

The crowd of English soldiers and Rouen civilians shouted and jeered at the Maid as she mounted an elevated platform to the stake directly over a huge pile of wood. She asked for a cross, so an English soldier fashioned two twigs from the wood pile into the shape of a small cross. Joan kissed it and placed this symbol near her heart against her breast in her robe. Then she suddenly asked that a crucifix be brought out so that she might gaze upon it during her ordeal. Friar Isambert ran into the church with the sacristan and came out to her with the processional cross, which she kissed and held for a few seconds. After the executioner had bound her hands behind her back around the stake, Friar Isambert lifted the crucifix high into the air so its corpus of the crucified Christ directly faced Joan.

Everything was ready to make her capital punishment more cruel than usual, with the wood piled high in such fashion as to burn her more slowly, thoroughly, and unmercifully. The executioner then placed his torch into the tinder at the bottom of the pile to start the fire. "When Joan saw the fire kindled she began to cry out in a loud voice 'Jesus, Jesus, Jesus!'"[138] She could see that Friar Isambert was too close to the flames, so for his safety she asked him to move with the processional crucifix farther away from the fire. The smoke started to choke her and the heat of the fire to sear her flesh. The Dominican friars Martin Ladvenu and Isambert de La Pierre testified: "We heard her from the midst of the fire calling on her Saints and her Archangel.... Then, as her head fell forward, in a sign that she was fervent in the faith of God, she gave a great cry of 'JESUS!'"[139]

---

[138] Pernoud, *Joan of Arc by Herself and Her Witnesses*, 232.
[139] Alice Buchon, *Joan of Arc and the Recovery of France*, ed. A. L. Rouse (New York: Macmillan, 1948), 226.

THE HEROIC MARTYR

The executioner stood there stupefied. Bedford ordered him to subdue the flames for the crowd to see that indeed the Maid was dead. Her singed, naked body, no longer covered by the penitential robe which had been consumed in the fire, revealed a woman with head bowed in apparent defeat and disgrace. The executioner restarted the fire so as to burn the rest of Joan's body to ashes. But Therage was unable to burn her heart and her intestines, "despite the oil, the sulfur, and the charcoal he applied."[140] He became greatly disturbed by the evident miracle and realized that he had executed a saint. Bedford ordered him then to take all the remains and ashes and dump them into the Seine River, which he did. The English regent wanted no French partisans to take anything as a possible relic.

Joan's pious invocations to God and her heroic disposition while dying had moved the hearts of nearly all in the crowd, including the hardened English soldiers and even some of the aristocrats. Witnesses reported that the secretary to the boy king of England, John Tressard, was afflicted with heavy grief, groaning and weeping lamentably over what he had seen and heard: "We are all lost, for we have burnt a good and holy person."[141] The widespread reaction among most people was that a great wrong and injustice had been done to the Maid of France. They went back to their homes in a somber and sorrowful mood. Therage, previously hateful and vengeful toward the Maid when lighting the fire, went later that day to an English Dominican, confessing that he had sinned gravely and that he repented of what he had done to Joan. He told the Dominican that at the very moment she expired and bowed her head in death, he saw "a white dove

---

[140] Pernoud, *Joan of Arc by Herself and Her Witnesses*, 234.
[141] Ibid., 233.

coming out [of the fire] on the side toward France." He also told Friar Isambert "that he greatly feared to be damned, for he had burnt a holy woman."[142] Another English soldier said that he had even seen the Holy Name of Jesus written glowingly across the flames.

One heart that was unmoved by the Maid's death was the very hard heart of the Burgundian bishop. His chicanery evidenced itself in the days following the execution. On the same afternoon of May 30, Friar Pierre Bosquier remarked that those who had judged and condemned Joan had done ill. For that remark, Cauchon sentenced him to a year in prison on bread and water. On June 7 Cauchon assembled some of the trial assessors to have them alter their sworn and signed statements of what Joan had said during the formal process and sequel. Guillaume (William) Manchon, as mentioned, was one of the few who refused to falsify his transcript or suborn his oath of office. Cauchon's henchmen Venderes, Courselles, Loiseleur, and Maurice, among others, had no qualms about participating in the bishop's deceit. Cauchon's charades continued on June 22, when he obtained for himself and his principal assessors "letters of warranty" from the king of England that would guarantee, on that king's authority, their immunity from any future legal proceedings or court trials, at the expense of the king of England. Cauchon's seared conscience moved him not to contrition but to more connivance as camouflage for his own misdeeds and injustices against the holy Maid.

---

[142] Pernoud, *Joan of Arc by Herself and Her Witnesses*, 234.

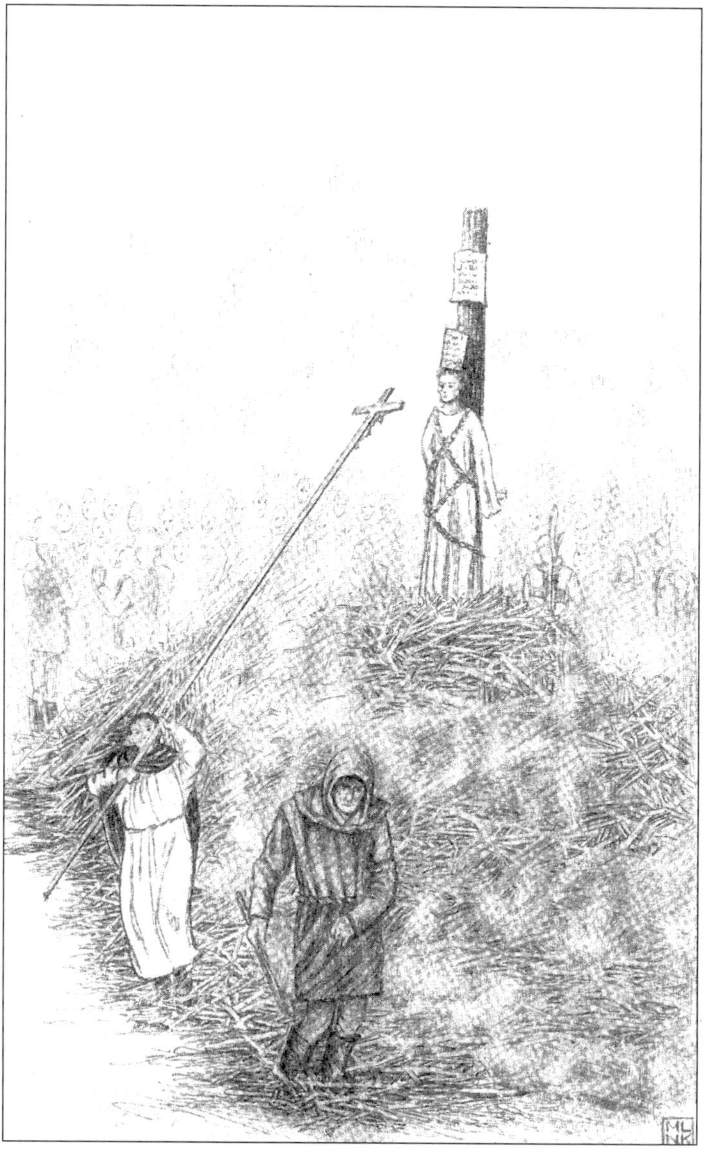

✣ Meditation ✣

FIDELITY IN LIFE AND IN DEATH

"Who among us can dwell with the devouring fire?
Who among us can dwell with everlasting burnings?"
He who walks righteously and speaks uprightly,
who despises the gain of oppressions.

—Isaiah 33:14–15

Now I will cry out like a woman in travail, I will gasp and pant.

—Isaiah 42:14

"Jesus!" Joan of Arc's last word was the Divine Word—Jesus, her Lord and her God. Jesus had always been the primary love of her life. Even in her youth, she realized that to please God she must do the heavenly Father's will, first in her active military mission and then in her imprisonment, trial, and death. That was the very purpose of Joan's being on this earth: to become like Christ Jesus in grace and mercy, in truth and charity. Her true self as a beloved virgin daughter of God who became a heroic martyr, a true witness, showed brilliantly in her death for Christ's sake. We can also hear in Joan's pardon of her persecutors a strong echo of Jesus' own words from the Cross: "Father, forgive them; for they know not what they do" (Luke 23:34). It was also an echo of the divine mercy exclaimed by the first Christian martyr, the young deacon Saint Stephen, as he was being stoned to death: "Lord Jesus, do not hold this sin against them!" (Acts 7:60). That merciful witness of Stephen won the graces from the glorified Christ Jesus for Saul's later conversion from persecutor of Christ in Christians to promoter of Christ among the Gentiles. The same echo of Jesus, the Divine Mercy, has sounded in the lives and deaths of Christian martyrs throughout the ages.

Our Lord Jesus Christ said, "[U]nless a grain of wheat falls into the earth and dies, it remains alone; but if it dies, it bears much fruit" (John 12:24). Jesus, the Good Seed of God, has died and risen in order to bear much fruit by the Holy Spirit in the lives of His saints, especially of His martyrs. "The blood of martyrs is the seed of Christians": this maxim expresses the triumph of the Holy Cross in Christianity's rapid growth amid persecutions and all attempts to suppress the gospel truth of God.

"Truth is worth pain and even conflict. I may not just accept a lie in order to have quiet. For it is not the first duty of a citizen, or of a Christian, to seek quiet; but rather it is that 'standing fast' by what is noble and great, which is what Christ has given us and which can reach as far as suffering, as far as a struggle that ends in martyrdom—and exactly in that way brings peace."[143]

The word *martyr* does not apply to everyone who suffers death, but only to those who die as witnesses and servants of divine Truth, Goodness, and Beauty, personified perfectly in the suffering Servant of God. "[H]e had no form or comeliness that we should look at him, and no beauty that we should desire him. He was despised and rejected by men; a man of sorrows, and acquainted with grief; and as one from whom men hide their faces he was despised, and we esteemed him not" (Isa. 53:2–3). Speaking several hundred years before Christ, the Jewish prophet had envisioned and described the Passion of the Messiah,

---

[143] Pope Benedict XVI in Peter John Cameron, ed., *Benedictus: Day by Day with Pope Benedict XVI* (San Francisco: Ignatius Press/Magnificat, 2006), 280.

the sufferings that the Servant of God would endure for the sins of his people. "Surely he has borne our griefs and carried our sorrows.... But he was wounded for our transgressions; he was bruised for our iniquities" (Isa. 53:4–5). Jesus the Messiah was—and is—the perfect Martyr in His witness of fidelity to God the Father and in His suffering service to humanity. Joan of Arc became like her beloved heavenly King and Lord Jesus, "perfect through suffering" (Heb. 2:10), by living and dying with the Holy Name of Jesus in her heart and on her lips.

Joan's heroic life demonstrated clearly her human, moral virtues as a true daughter of France. Yet her heroic death reveals more brilliantly her divine, supernatural virtues as a true daughter of God. "It is ... fundamental to our concept of Joan's heroism that she died to testify to her truthfulness."[144] "Wanting to be a French soldier, a leader of men into combat, [Joan went] from her simple life in Domrémy to the king in Chinon and Reims, to the battlefields and siege sites of Orléans, Jargeau, Meung, Beaugency, Patay, Saint Denis, Saint Pierre-le-Moutier, La Charité, Senlis, Crepy-en-Valois, Melun, Compiègne, and finally to the tribunal and then the stake at Rouen."[145] "Whatever the course of our lives, we should receive them as the highest gift from the hand of God, in which equally reposed the power to do nothing whatever for us. Indeed, we should accept misfortune, not only in thanks, but in infinite gratitude to Providence, which by such means detaches us from an excessive love for earthly things and elevates our minds to the celestial and divine."[146]

---

[144] Marina Warner, *Joan of Arc: The Image of Female Heroism* (New York: Alfred A. Knopf, 1981), 272.

[145] DeVries, *Joan of Arc: A Military Leader*, 7.

[146] Galileo Galilei in his personal reflections late in life after being silenced by the pope for his astronomical observations.

VI

The Nation Reborn

*Blessed is the nation whose God is the L*ORD*,
the people whom he has chosen as his heritage!*

—Psalm 33:12

Open the gates, that the righteous nation which keeps faith may enter in. Thou [O God] dost keep him in perfect peace, whose mind is stayed on thee, because he trusts in thee.

—Isaiah 26:2–3

Be subject for the Lord's sake to every human institution, whether it be to the emperor as supreme, or to governors as sent by him to punish those who do wrong and to praise those who do right.

—1 Peter 2:13–14

✠

The End of an Enemy Alliance

Bedford with his English soldiers and their Burgundian allies had rid themselves of the dreaded and hated Maid of France by condemning her through a Church tribunal as a heretic and sorceress, then executing her. He had to regain the military initiative in his campaign to defeat and discredit King Charles and establish English hegemony over all of France. The regent Bedford realized that to discredit Charles further, he had to get his nephew Henry VI, the boy king of England, also crowned in France. Yet, Reims was no longer accessible, either to Duke Philip of Burgundy or to Duke John of Bedford. Two years before, the people there had witnessed the magnificent royal anointing and coronation of Charles VII in a centuries-old French tradition. The citizens of Reims had become solidly loyal to their true French king.

So Bedford brought his nephew to the cathedral of Notre Dame in Paris, a city that his English soldiers controlled, to be anointed and crowned a few days before Christmas 1431 by the boy's great-uncle Cardinal Beaufort. The hastily prepared, unceremonious liturgy was performed not by a French archbishop, according to tradition, but by the English cardinal in a rite previously performed only in England. Thus, Bedford failed to achieve his aim of winning popular support from the Parisians for his nephew. Furthermore, once the ceremony at Notre Dame concluded, Beaufort demanded, in the boy Henry's presence, that his nephew Bedford resign as regent. The English royal family feud began to undermine the unity of purpose of English adventures into France.

Another rupture occurred a year or so later, when Bedford's wife, Anne of Burgundy, died, and Bedford very soon remarried the wealthy Jacquetta of Luxembourg. Bedford thereby seriously offended his former brother-in-law, Philip of Burgundy, on two counts: first, the marriage took place so soon after his sister Anne's death; and second, Bedford did not seek Philip's approval, inasmuch as the new wife was from Luxembourg, a vassal principality of Burgundy. The personal rift between the two dukes eventually led to the political unraveling of Burgundy's alliance with England.[147]

An additional negative factor for Bedford was his lack of financial resources and manpower to implement his war plans vigorously. Although his field commander, Talbot, newly ransomed from the French, was back in action in 1434, recapturing numerous towns in Normandy, nevertheless the estates in that province could not raise enough funds to sustain military operations. Peasant unrest and revolts in Caen and Bayeaux further threatened English control over those lands. Then, as Philip of Burgundy began to recognize the increasing popular support among the French people for his cousin Charles and the simultaneous waning of English fortunes in France, he and Tremoille, formerly King Charles VII's closest adviser, proposed

---

[147] Wilson-Smith, *Joan of Arc: Maid, Myth and History*, 91.

peace negotiations among the main belligerents. Bedford himself, suffering from a terminal illness in Rouen, could not attend the talks, which began in August 1435. His uncle, Cardinal Beaufort, went as the political representative for England.

The agreed meeting place was the main abbey in Arras, a prosperous Franco-Flemish town in the territory of Duke Philip of Burgundy, who hosted the peace conference. Two cardinals presided—one sent by the pope from Rome, the other by the schismatic Council of Basel. The Roman pontiff wanted the Christian peoples of England, France, and Burgundy to settle their internal and international differences and to combine their military forces against the Ottoman Turks assaulting Constantinople. King Charles VII, desirous of personal reconciliation with his cousin, agreed to Philip's peace overtures and sent his representative to Arras. But Beaufort rejected any sort of compromise on England's territorial claims in France. He and the French envoy refused to be together in the same room with each other, even in the same chapel. In early September Beaufort abruptly left the conference, which consequently excluded England from any benefit from a peace settlement.

Reconciliation among Frenchmen

One week later Bedford died and was buried in the cathedral of Rouen, still an English stronghold. Another week or so after Bedford's death, Charles and Philip signed the Treaty of Arras, effectively ending the civil war in France and returning Burgundy to its historical connection with France and Philip to fealty under France's true king. As part of their reconciliation, Charles agreed to a formal apology for his former associates who had killed Philip's father years before. A few well-placed bribes also pacified some of the dissenting aristocratic vassals of Philip, whose profitable trade with England would otherwise be adversely affected.[148] Just a few days after the formal signing of the Arras accord in late September, Isabeau of Bavaria, the mother of King Charles, died in Paris. Hers was the last death of the principal actors in the Treaty of Troyes, which gave France to England. Nullifying the old one, the new treaty gave France back to the French!

The Treaty of Arras in 1435 would have offered very generous terms to the English, former allies of the Burgundians, enabling them to keep most of Normandy and some other parts of France. But after Bedford's death and Beaufort's obstinacy, King Henry VI of England, still too immature and ill-advised, refused to concede his rule over France or to relinquish any part of the colonial empire that his father, Henry V, had gained by military force at Agincourt and by the subsequent Treaty of Troyes. Thus, the English refused the terms of the Treaty of Arras, prolonging the Hundred Years' War. Back in Paris, still garrisoned by English troops, Henry VI, with yet another uncle as his regent, demanded that all Parisians swear allegiance to England, the consummate cultural insult to the proud Parisians.

By 1436, after a harsh winter and deprivation by their English overlords, the common people of Paris thwarted the safe passage of English troops and forced them to retreat into the Bastille fortress, while chasing English lackeys among the University of Paris clergy into monasteries. French partisans also lowered ladders over the outer walls to permit entry into the city by French soldiers prepared for the assault. The French commander de Richemont, on behalf of King Charles VII, proclaimed a general pardon and amnesty to all Parisians. He also offered new and fair

---

[148] Wilson-Smith, *Joan of Arc: Maid, Myth and History*, 88.

THE NATION REBORN

terms for the English to leave Paris, and eventually all of France, which they accepted. In 1437, less than six years after his nephew Henry's pseudocoronation there, King Charles VII of France made his triumphant entry into the capital city and its cathedral of Notre Dame. Meanwhile, the provinces pledged their loyalty to their newly empowered king. With the imposition of permanent taxes for a standing army, the restored nation of France was to be defended and governed by an absolute monarch.

England had become enfeebled by internal quarrels among its own aristocrats and by the expenses of war on the Continent. In 1441 King Charles himself led the reconquest of Normandy. As his army advanced, however, he allowed his vengeful soldiers to throw three hundred English prisoners naked into the Seine River to be drowned. By 1450 Rouen, the city of Joan's martyrdom, became free of the English during the Britanny campaign. Count John Dunois, formerly known as the Bastard of Orléans, was by then the French king's lieutenant general and viewed the victory. Soon thereafter the first royal inquiry convened to examine the legality of the 1431 trial that condemned the Maid to death.

By 1452 King Charles's forces won Guyenne and Gascony, and then the Bordeaux region surrendered to him. Charles VII had also won a new name—Charles the Very Victorious. His military campaigns succeeded in reestablishing the ancient lands of the kingdom of France and in reaffirming his own legitimacy as ruler of that nation under God in the Church. King Charles reconvened the official investigation into the condemnation trial, with the elderly, frail Isabelle Romée also petitioning Church and state to redress the grievances against her daughter: "But certain enemies had her arraigned in a religious trial. Despite her disclaimers and appeals, both tacit and expressed, and without any help given to her defense, she was put through a perfidious, violent, iniquitous, and sinful trial. The judges condemned her falsely, damnably, and criminally, and put her to death in a cruel manner by fire. I demand that her name be restored!"[149] That same fiery spirit which had characterized the beloved daughter Jeannette was still burning intensely in the heart of the old mother, Isabelle Romée.

The first theological expert contributing his viewpoint at the opening session was the French bishop Elie de Bourdeilles: "This girl, I say, was sent for the liberation and consolation of the king and the kingdom ... and in service of God she liberated the kingdom from the said English, with God compassionately consenting, as one can piously believe.... Since she did not have this wisdom by nature or by occupation, it is fitting, as it seems, that she had it from grace; and thus it can be considered that it was from God, with the presupposition ... that she never acted against justice, nor was she persuaded by human affection, but led only by zeal for justice."[150]

The cleric Massieu, who had been present next to Joan in the Ouen cemetery, also testified: "From what I saw, I believe that the proceedings were not taken for the honor of God and of the Catholic Faith, but in order to bring dishonor to the King of France."[151] He and six other witnesses present on May 24, 1431, including the Rouen trial court clerk Manchon, gave their sworn testimonies at the rehabilitation proceedings, exposing the dis-

---

[149] Spoto, *Joan: The Mysterious Life of the Heretic Turned Saint*, 198.
[150] Jane Marie Pinzino, "Speaking of Angels—A Fifteenth Century Bishop in Defense of Joan of Arc's Mystical Voices," in Bonnie Wheeler and Charles T. Wood, eds., *Fresh Verdicts on Joan of Arc* (New York: Garland Publishing, 1996), 165, 167.
[151] Robo, *Saint Joan: The Woman and the Saint*, 123.

honesty of Pierre Cauchon and his English conspirators: "What Joan signed was a paper of no more than eight lines, saying that she would not again bear arms, wear men's clothing, or cut her hair. That was what I read to her. But another document, not this one, was put into the trial record. She had no idea of what was on it, nor the consequences of signing it."[152]

Restoring the good name of Jeanne La Pucelle was obviously very important to King Charles VII for his political purposes and to Lady Isabelle Romée du Lys for her personal reasons. But for France as a nation, the "rehabilitation" of Joan of Arc was essential to national identity and social integrity. The people of France could hope for a benevolent king to rule them in peace and prosperity for their time on earth; but for lasting happiness, they themselves needed spiritual renewal.

---

[152] Spoto, *Joan: The Mysterious Life of the Heretic Turned Saint*, 183.

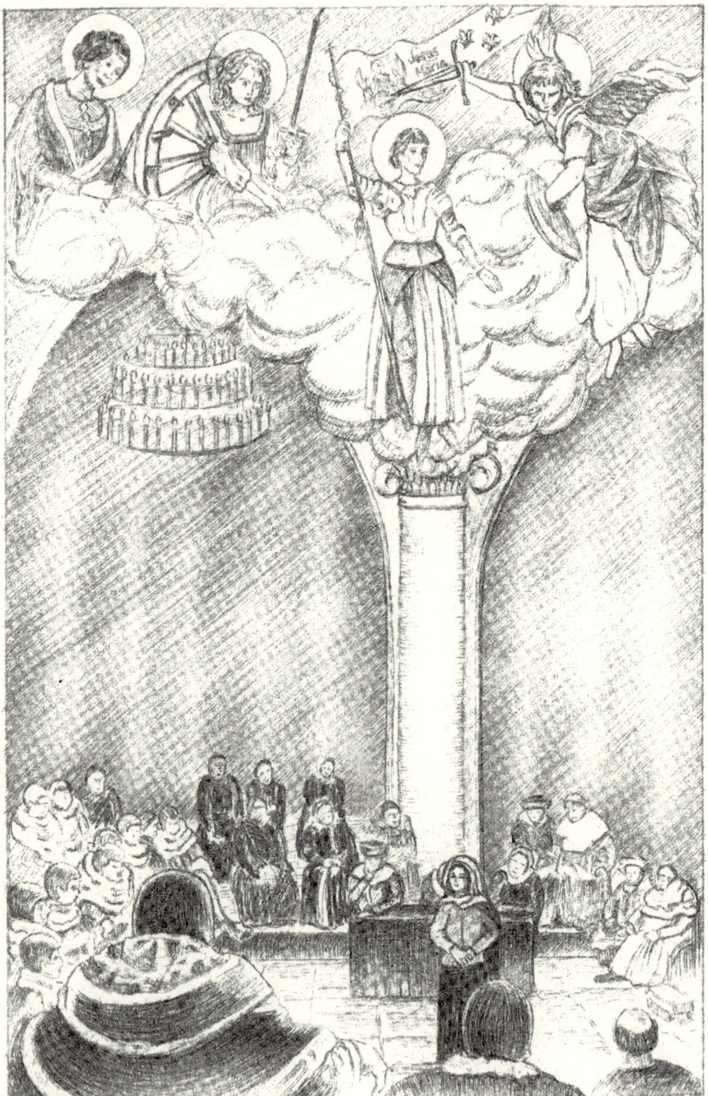
Maria

THE NATION REBORN

⚜ Meditation ⚜

A VIRGIN MOTHERING A NATION

"France might have been England at this day, instead of a republic, under the rule of King George and, following the temperament and tendency of those days, the entire population speaking English; for by royal decree, France, as a distinct nation in tongue, customs, laws, and looks, could have been erased. That is, in brief, the effect of Joan of Arc's life on the world."[153]

In that late medieval era when Joan of Arc left Domrémy for Vaucouleurs to ask Baudricourt for a military escort to meet the dauphin Charles, she told him she must "go into France." She knew that the kingdom of France had already splintered into various warring principalities during the course of the wars with England, and that Burgundy had become an enemy of France because of its alliance with England, the unjust aggressor nation. Because of aristocratic rivalries and longtime civil unrest, most Frenchmen had little sense of a national identity; instead, a more provincial or even parochial outlook prevailed. They would have considered themselves as Burgundians, Armagnacs, Parisians, Normans, or the like and sworn loyalty to their regional duke or to the one who had the most powerful army to protect them and not destroy them. Charles VII had inherited a dissolute and bankrupt kingdom from his feeble-minded father and his traitorous mother; he had serious self-doubts about his own legitimacy to rule; and he commanded no widespread

---

[153] American Numismatic Society, *Joan of Arc Loan Exhibition Catalogue*, 7, for a 1913 exhibit in New York City.

respect from his subjects to motivate and lead an army for a fight to win the nation's wars—until Almighty God sent him a young woman who could!

Although King Charles VII did not show much appreciation for his greatest benefactor during her lifetime, he was certainly influenced by La Pucelle. On the march to Reims, Charles offered gracious terms and amnesty to all the cities and towns along the way. Joan had appealed to Philip of Burgundy to be reconciled with his cousin Charles and attend his coronation in Reims. Even though Philip did not attend and continued in animosity for several more years, Charles still desired a real peace between them and their subjects, although he was indeed naive and gullible in following Tremoille's advice to trust Philip, instead of heeding Joan's counsel to march quickly toward Paris to defeat the English. Charles realized only after Joan's death that the simple Maid had shown him heavenly wisdom by her good counsel: that bold action, not timidity, would ensure social justice and prosperity in the realm of France; that only forgiveness, magnanimity, and reconciliation between factions and within God's Church would bring peace to the souls of the king and his people; that only a nation of firm purpose and trust in Almighty God could maintain that peace and tranquillity at home and abroad. All her earlier prophesies had been fulfilled. It became obvious that the Maid in Heaven was still inspiring France's king and countrymen to restore themselves as a nation under God.

In Joan of Arc's own time and into our modern times, many commentators have marveled at how the demoralized and divided peoples of France under a timid, unattractive, self-centered, indecisive king were eventually restored as a nation because the Maid had entered their scene. Her virtuous character, iron will, bold decisiveness, indomitable courage, and religious fervor profoundly transformed the French people and their king. Once she appeared, her men-at-arms no longer feared a fight with the English. Instead, they would fight to the death because they were in God's good graces and shared Joan's conviction that the liberation of their country was a just cause, willed by God Himself. The "loser" dauphin became the "very victorious" king mainly because of the "very virtuous" virgin, even after the departure of her soul from amid the flames at Rouen "in the form of a dove toward France." The virgin of hinterland Domrémy became the mother of mainland France by her fiery labor of love.

From his boyhood, Samuel Clemens was fascinated with the figure of Joan of Arc. Only in later life, after his tales written with the pseudonym Mark Twain had made him famous, did he spend twelve years researching and writing about her, which gave him the most pleasure of any of his literary works. He concluded his own labor of love with this paragraph:

> I have finished my story of Joan of Arc, that wonderful child, that sublime personality, that spirit which in one regard has had no peer and will have none—this: its purity from all alloy of self-seeking, self-interest, personal ambition. In it no trace of these motives can be found, search as you may, and this cannot be said of any other person whose name appears in profane history. With Joan of Arc love of country was more than a sentiment—it was a passion. She was the Genius of Patriotism—she was Patriotism embodied, concreted, made flesh, and palpable to the touch and visible to the eye. Love, Mercy, Charity, Fortitude, War, Peace, Poetry, Music—these may be

symbolized as any shall prefer: by figures of either sex, of any age; but a slender girl in her first young bloom, with the martyr's crown upon her head, and in her hand the sword that severed her country's bonds—shall not this, and no other, stand for PATRIOTISM for all the ages until time shall end?[154]

The ambassador of France at Washington, DC, wrote a letter to an American gentleman in New York in 1912, extolling the character of Joan of Arc:

The heroine of the France of the past and the France of today—the simple, valorous, clear-sighted, ready-witted, impassioned girl of Lorraine, who awakened a great country from an almost deadly sleep, changed the course of history; died as she had lived, a model for men and women of all time; winning the admiration of friend and foe alike; and descrying that all think of her who never thought of herself; as modest at the head of armies as she was pasturing her sheep; and leaving in the brief space of a nineteen-year life a record with which no other can compare.[155]

Certainly that early twentieth-century French ambassador to the United States would speak most highly of his own country's greatest patriot. Much more impressive is the degree of admiration for Joan of Arc expressed so lavishly by a young Englishman who became Great Britain's prime minister during World War II, the inspirational Winston Churchill:

[154] Samuel Langhorn Clemens (Mark Twain), from the conclusion of his last book, *Joan of Arc*.
[155] *Joan of Arc Loan Exhibition Catalogue*, 23.

THE NATION REBORN

Joan was a being so uplifted from the ordinary run of mankind that she finds no equal in a thousand years! The records of her trial present us with facts alive today through all the mists of time. Out of her own mouth can she be judged in [every] generation. She embodied the natural goodness and valor of the human race in unexampled perfection. Unconquerable courage, infinite compassion, the virtue of the simple, the wisdom of the just—shone forth in her. She glorifies as she freed the soil from which she sprang. All soldiers should read her story and ponder on the words and deeds of the true warrior.[156]

"It could be said that since there is no more feudalism, nor are there powerful kings because rulers do not settle their differences by marrying their daughters to their enemies, and peasant girls have ceased to approach heads of state with revelations from God, the lessons of the Hundred Years War, whatever they might be, are no longer relevant. But as long as political power, sovereignty, national identity, and war are pertinent, and as long as traits such as honor, pride, glory, greed, envy, hatred, and revenge are part of human nature, the Hundred Years War remains entirely relevant.... Joan seems to have recognized, better than most, a special historical circumstance that was prolonging the war, that the era in which the English presence in France would be tolerated had drawn to a close. It was Joan who told the English they had no right in France and backed it up with military action that to *her* was a pure expression of divine will."[157]

---

[156] Winston Churchill, *History of the English Speaking Peoples*, vol. 1.
[157] Fraioli, *Joan of Arc and the Hundred Years War*, 71, 74.

A truly patriotic recognition and love of one's own national identity is not equivalent to nationalism, nor is it compatible with the extreme attitudes of chauvinism and jingoism. To consider one's own nation as superior to all others or to foster an aggressive militarism for exploitation of other nations is actually a vice, not the virtue of patriotism. True patriots support their own countrymen, while also respecting the rights of people from other cultures and nationalities. A nation forms from local and regional communities sharing a common language, customs, commerce, system of government, and spiritual, moral, and religious ideals and practices. The United States of America can be called a nation of nationalities, from the diversity of its people: *e pluribus unum*—"out of many, one" nation under God.

The French people have continuously celebrated their heroine's victories, but have they continuously imitated her virtues? If the French could see a new embodiment of true patriotism in their national heroine, they should also recognize and practice her true religion. Modern nations have written constitutions and systems of laws for order and peace in society and the administration of justice among the citizens. Both within nations and in relationships among nation-states, citizens and their governments must transcend nationalism and abide by universal principles of mutual respect and cooperation, in order that societies might enjoy prosperity and peace on this earth. Only a worldwide organization that seeks no economic gain or political power for itself, but rather serves the cause of justice and peace on earth can transcend nationalism and build an international, interdependent community of nations. That selfless servant organization is the universal Church.

Pope Pius XII, who led the Catholic Church through the horrors of World War II and its aftermath, gave a strong exhortation about the immorality of wars of aggression and the punitive threat of a United Nations intervention upon such aggressors.

> It is with the force of reason, not of armaments, that Justice makes its advance. And empires not founded on Justice are not blessed by God. A policy emancipated from morality betrays those who want it so. Nothing is lost with peace. Everything may be lost with war! Let men come again to understand one another. Negotiating with good will and with respect for their reciprocal rights, they will perceive that honorable success is never precluded to sincere and constructive negotiations. May it please the Almighty that the voice of this Father of the (worldwide) Christian family, of this Servant of servants who, unworthily indeed but really, brings among men the Person of Jesus Christ, His word and authority, may find a prompt and willing acceptance in minds and hearts. Let the strong hear us; we entreat them through the Blood of Christ, whose conquering force in the world was meekness in life and death. With us is that Christ who of brotherly love made His Commandment fundamental, solemn, the substance of His religion, the promise of salvation for individuals and nations.[158]

In a 1965 address to the general assembly of the United Nations, Pope Paul VI made an impassioned appeal to the member nations: "No more war! War never again!" He was expressing the perennial hope of the Church, as popes before and after him

---

[158] Pope Pius XII, quoted in *Society and Politics*, a collection of writings and addresses by Pope Pius XII on various subjects, published by the Holy See, 324–325.

have. Yet the same Pope Paul insisted repeatedly in the course of his pontificate from 1963 to 1978 that "if you want peace, work for justice; if you want peace, respect Life!" "The Holy See believes that international law is essential to the maintenance of peace among nations. When peace breaks down, international law setting limits on the conduct of warfare is essential to the re-establishment of an enduring peace and civilized life at war's end. International law governing the conduct of warfare is known as the law of armed conflict. More recently it is referred to as 'international humanitarian law.' International law and the Church's just war principles have always recognized that limitation and proportionality must be respected in warfare."[159]

---

[159] Archbishop Francis Chullikat, the Holy See's permanent observer to the UN, in a July 2011 talk in Kansas City, Missouri, addressing "The Nuclear Question: The Church's Teachings and the Current State of Affairs."

VII

The Church Renewed

Better than this is childlessness with virtue, for in the memory of virtue is immortality, because it is known both by God and by men. When it is present, men imitate it, and they long for it when it has gone; and throughout all time it marches crowned in triumph, victor in the contest for prizes that are undefiled.

—Wisdom 4:1–2

I know your works, your toil and your patient endurance, and how you . . . have tested those who call themselves apostles but are not, and found them to be false . . . But I have this against you, that you have abandoned the love you had at first. . . . [R]epent and do the works you did at first.

—Revelation 2:2, 4, 5

⚜

Healing among Clergy and Laity

The "rehabilitation" tribunal process, known also as the "nullification" trial, began its first session in March 1450, reconvened in 1452, and concluded by May 1456. Slowly healing wounds in relationships among churchmen as with statesmen and among the provincial populations added to the difficult, painful process of reconciliation within the Church in the kingdom of France, still being reunited by the "very victorious" king in the middle of the fifteenth century. After all, England and France had been at war with each other for most of the past hundred years, and the Burgundians and Armagnacs within France had been in a blood feud for several decades, only recently resolved by a pledge of loyalty to King Charles from the Duke of Burgundy after Charles's victories. The various factions of clergy too were still highly politicized. So what was begun for political and personal reasons by the French king as recognized head of state must be concluded for religious and spiritual reasons by the Catholic pope as visible head of the Church on earth — the Church Militant.

One of the most serious and continuing theological controversies, relevant to the condemnation trial and affecting also the rehabilitation process, was the contention by many clerics from the University of Paris that a Church council, which they and their academically credentialed bishops convened apart from the pope, was superior in authority to the Roman pontiff. The intellectually proud "theologians" from Paris had been proponents of the invalid Council of Basel at one point and of the antipope in Avignon at another time. Moreover, their sycophancy to the English was obvious throughout the condemnation trial. Even those reputed theologians who were not bishops considered themselves intellectually superior to bishops and clergy from the mendicant orders, such as the Franciscans and the Dominicans, who promoted a popular religiosity among the country folk, unlike the sophisticated Parisians. After all, one of their club members, Pierre Cauchon, had arrogated to himself the authority to judge Joan of Arc, to refuse her canonical right of appeal to the pope, and to overrule and punish those clergy who objected to his unjust actions. The questions of papal authority in relation to other bishops, individually or collectively, and of the magisterial teaching authority of the pope with the bishops in relation to other clergy, religious, and the laypeople of God were not fully answered.

As successors of Christ's apostles and enlightened by the Holy Spirit, bishops then as always have had Christ's divine authority and responsibility to discern spirits (cf. 1 Cor. 12:10), good ones from evil ones, and to teach the whole gospel of Christ in matters of faith and morals that affect the lives of God's people, correcting and reproving the errant ones. Addressed both by the judges in the former trial of condemnation and by those in the new tribunal sessions, the central spiritual and theological question was whether Joan of Arc had challenged and rejected that divine authority of the Church and had substituted her own private revelations as superior to divine revelation, taught unerringly by the pope and the bishops. The question of the Maid's heresy or fidelity, her sorcery or her sanctity, must be answered correctly to ensure the future credibility of the Catholic Church, both in France and throughout the world. Was Joan a heretical sorceress or a faithful saint?

The 1431 Church tribunal, under English political and military control at Rouen, condemned Joan as a deceitful fabricator of divine revelations, attributing her Voices to the Devil rather than to Saints Michael the Archangel, Catherine of Alexandria, and Margaret of Antioch. The second Church tribunal, under French political and military control, set out to annul the first tribunal and vindicate both Joan and her king, Charles VII, as true successor, by the grace of God, to the throne and kingdom of France. The rehabilitation tribunal process sought testimonies in Joan's favor, examined the condemnation tribunal's irregular technical and canonical procedures, and determined for faithful Christians their legitimate forms of devotion in addition to Holy Mass.

The subsequent sessions of the rehabilitation process from 1452 to 1456 were no longer directed by the clergy of France, but by Pope Nicholas V's envoy, Guillaume d'Estouteville, a prelate at Rome in service of the Holy See. D'Estouteville was also related to King Charles by a grandmother, who was a sister of Charles V, the king's grandfather. Because the condemnation of Joan involved the Inquisition, canonical procedure required the presence of the General Inquisitor for France, John Brehal, who earnestly undertook that mission to its completion. D'Estouteville, later called to Paris on other papal business, appointed Philippe de La Rose, treasurer of the Rouen cathedral, to represent him at the interrogation of witnesses, assisting Brehal.[160]

Brehal and de la Rose expanded the scope of the original questionnaire to have witnesses answer some of the following issues: (1) English hatred of Joan and constraints on her judges, especially the threats and pressure exerted on the officers of the court; (2) the lack of a defense counselor for her, contrary to law; (3) her illegal detention in a secular prison; (4) deceitful methods and manner of interrogation used to incite her to oppose the Church authorities; (5) Joan's true attitudes, piety, and submissiveness toward the pope and the Church; (6) subterfuge in using the term *Church Militant*, of which she was ignorant; (7) the lack of agreement between the official Latin transcript circulated by Cauchon and the French text of Manchon and two other recorders of the condemnation trial; (8) the incompetence of the judges; (9) the anomaly of granting a supposed heretic the last sacraments; (10) Joan's dispositions during her final moments; (11) the real motives of the case; and (12) public notoriety of these facts.[161]

Bishop Elie de Bourdeilles, one of the principal prelates at the initial theological presentations, focused his attention on Joan's testimonies, private revelations, and personal religious devotions. He saw her as a true daughter of God, of the Church, and of France. The bishop also elaborated on the activities of angels in the lives of human beings: "We say that angelic spirits are soldiers of God, because we know that they contend against higher powers, though they fight battles not with toil but with

---

[160] Pernoud, *The Retrial of Joan of Arc*, 20, 25–28.
[161] Ibid., 33–34.

authority; for whatever they do, they attack the impure." He noted that the work of every guardian angel is: (1) to safeguard the human soul from sin; (2) to promote and instruct that person in morality (virtuous living); (3) to reveal the divine will for him or her; and (4) to preserve virginity or chastity in the willing soul.[162]

Many clergy and laity, aristocrats, soldiers, and peasants, from all regions of France, including those who had opposed her, testified about their contacts with Joan the Maid from her youth to her army life through her imprisonment, trial, and execution. Her three main clergy antagonists were already dead: the deceitful Burgundian bishop Pierre Cauchon died suddenly in a barber's chair while being shaved; the foul-mouthed, vicious prosecutor John d'Estivet was found dead, his body rotting in a street gutter; and the lying deputy Nicholas Midy died wretchedly of leprosy. One of Joan's main condemnation trial opponents at the nullification "retrial" was John Beaupere, still hostile toward and contemptuous of Joan for her inspired response to his devilish attempt to trap her about being in a state of grace. With his pride still wounded after his humiliation by the Maid more than twenty years earlier, he called her "very subtle, with a woman's subtlety." Another enemy, Thomas de Courcelles, who had previously voted with Midy for the torture treatment of Joan in prison, feigned ignorance or absence from some of the 1431 sessions in order to cloak his previous hostility to the Maid. Although he obviously evaded certain questions and lied during the retrial, his shrewd politicking, excellent rhetorical skills, and academic training later won him the prestigious position of rector at the University of Paris.

---

[162] Pinzino, "Speaking of Angels," 168.

All other tribunal witnesses corroborated Joan's exemplary virtues throughout her life, from childhood to soldiering to imprisonment, condemnation, and death. Even the friend of the Luxembourg duke, the knight Haimond de Macy, who had attempted to fondle the Maid's breasts at the Beaurevoir castle, testified to her strong rebuff of his impure sexual advances. Evidently repentant at the time of the retrial for that previous misconduct, he testified also to the mockery of Joan in her prison cell in Warwick's castle at Rouen by several of the aristocrats at the dinner party he had attended. His honesty revealed that the graces and mercies of God were purifying his own heart and soul because of the intercession of the saintly Maid.

The Triumph of Holiness

In 1456 from Rome, Pope Calixtus III revoked the Rouen sentence against Joan of Arc and nullified the original 1431 trial proceedings that had unjustly condemned her. The pope vigorously declared: "The actions of Joan are worthy of admiration rather than condemnation [and] the former judgment, in form as well as in principles, deserves to be reprehended and detested."[163] "Reprehended and detested" — the pope thereby explicitly censured Joan's chief condemnation judge, the deceased, corrupt former bishop of Beauvais and Lisieux. Some chroniclers report that, immediately after the pope had nullified and condemned the 1431 Rouen trial, certain French partisans dug up Pierre Cauchon's rotten corpse and threw it into a drain!

The resolution of Joan of Arc's case brought peace and unity to France, but it did not resolve other serious problems facing the Church beyond that nation's borders. The Catholic Church

---

[163] Robo, *Saint Joan: The Woman and the Saint*, 134.

still needed an internal reformation in canonical procedures and pastoral practices as well as an interior renewal in the spirituality of the clergy and religious orders and in their relationship to the lay faithful. Unfortunately, political considerations by churchmen continued to dominate Church decisions. Although the Great Western Schism also had been resolved in principle, its negative practical effects on the Church remained, along with the disruptions and disunity caused by the Hundred Years' War and other international conflicts among Christian nations. Church and state disruptions in the West had tragic repercussions also for Byzantine Christians in the East, still alienated from Rome by schism and by memories of past abuses by Latins.

Constantinople, a previously great city like Rome or Paris, had been built in the sixth century over ancient Byzantium into a magnificent Christian religious and cultural center combining Greek and Oriental architecture, art, and customs. The city suffered terribly under derelict Latin Christian soldiers during the Fourth Crusade in 1204. The army of Michael VIII Palaeologus conquered the Latins in 1261 and restored the Byzantine Empire, bringing its culture back also to the capital city, although never to its former grandeur. Parts of the city had been falling into ruins when Ottoman sultans ascended to power and began assaulting the strongholds of Byzantine Christianity. With no help from pope or kings or their armies from the West, Constantinople fell to the Ottoman Turks in May 1453. Among the tens of thousands killed was the Christian emperor, whose body the Muslims beheaded; they then paraded his head around the city like a trophy. The Turks also slaughtered many innocent women and children during their rampage. They desecrated all Christian churches by turning them into mosques, including the once magnificent Church of Hagia Sophia (Holy Wisdom).[164] The Ottomans completed their rout of Greek Byzantine Christianity and would try for four more centuries to extend their empire by wars against other Christian nations in the West.

The Church had "rehabilitated" Joan of Arc by nullifying and condemning the injustice done to her. Yet the Church would delay Joan's "exaltation" at Catholic altars for several more centuries. The Latin Church faced another more immediate challenge to her institutional authority by a new individualism expressed first in the Renaissance of art, architecture, science, and culture, and then even in politics and religion. Albeit with the patronage of prelates and princes, independent study, artistry, scientific inquiry and such endeavors gave rise to individual self-expression, certainly enhancing Western culture in a revival of the Greco-Roman style. But that individualism also led to a notion of supremacy of the individual over the community, of self-interest and self-determination independent of the common good of the community or of the nation or even of the Church. The individual's conscience could reign supreme, even when the individual rejected certain truths of Christian Faith already defined by the Church. Less than a century after Joan of Arc's death, many European nations divided their loyalties toward Church and state and thus lost their shared heritage of Christian unity and universality. Fierce contentions between Protestant Reformers and Catholic counterreformers began.

The widespread moral corruption of many high clergymen and religious orders scandalized most Christians, whose righteous indignation demanded their protestations. The misconduct of

---

[164] Bunson, *Encyclopedia of Catholic History*, 227.

Catholics, however, was further compounded by the greed of aristocrats, especially in Northern Europe far from Rome. Those powerful noblemen saw the opportunity within their nations to seize land and property that was held in common by religious communities. They would support any prominent Protestant preacher, even one espousing heresy, in order to expropriate the desired religious land holdings for themselves. Hostility among Christians of opposing sensibilities and affiliations persisted because of "rugged individualism" and self-righteous rejection of Church authority on matters of faith and morals.

The tumult and suffering throughout Europe caused by religious and cultural wars, among Christian nations and also with Islamic countries, intensified again because of periodic outbreaks of the dreaded bubonic plague. Then, by the eighteenth century, some French intellectuals began their cultural introspection known as the Enlightenment, whose philosophers and literary figures were actually formulating another version of individual superiority by elevating human reason over divine faith. The false dichotomy they presented between faith and reason in the human search for truth, goodness, and beauty fostered an antiauthority, antireligious cynicism among many of their fellow disgruntled countrymen, by then enduring social and economic stagnation and cultural malaise. Extravagance by French kings, whose legitimacy was still directly connected with the Catholic Church, when contrasted with the abject poverty among many French citizens created the sure recipe for revolution.

The French Revolution of 1789, with its slogan of "liberty, equality, and fraternity," was the result, not of true enlightenment leading to authentic human freedom, equality, and brotherhood, but of an intellectual darkness leading to a Reign of Terror. The terrorists did not stop after they killed the French king and queen and their aristocratic supporters; they went after clergymen and religious women who refused to pledge allegiance to their hateful, murderous regime, which opposed the Church of God. Among the many places outside Paris, the terrorists went to Compiègne, where Joan of Arc had been captured. There they arrested the humble, prayerful, cloistered Carmelite nuns, then brought them back to Paris for execution. Novices and longtime professed Sisters alike sang their prayers in unison as each was killed by guillotine, one by one until the mother superior's solo voice was silenced. Surely those blessed nuns received heavenly comfort from their sister martyr Joan, as she had been comforted by her sister martyrs Catherine and Margaret.

The end of the French monarchy meant also the end of cooperation between state and Church in France. Even after Napoleon Bonaparte established military rule and executed the principal terrorists, Church-state relations did not improve. The brilliant but arrogant little general led his army around Europe, defeating other nations and ransacking their economies to feed and feast his own troops. His soldiers went so far as to steal gold from the churches along his warpaths. But the people of Malta, an island nation originally evangelized by Saint Paul himself, outwitted Napoleon and his men. Being very proud of their beautifully gilded and ornate parish churches, yet not wanting to tempt the French marauders, the Maltese used darkened paint to cover the gold and hid many religious ornaments from the invaders. So Napoleon went on to Rome, where he imprisoned and harassed the Roman pontiff for opposing his unjust aggression. That self-crowned, self-serving, short-statured, unholy emperor even misused the revered memory of Joan of Arc for his own pompous and nationalistic political purposes, by having commemorative coins minted with his image on one side and hers on the other. Finally, Napoleon met ultimate defeat at Waterloo and was exiled to the island of Elba.

For much of the nineteenth century, insurrections, economic deprivation, and social unrest continued to disrupt life in France. Nevertheless, the people of Orléans and their bishops could not and would not ever forget their beloved Jeanne La Pucelle. They continued to celebrate their heroic liberator. "I like the peasant simplicity in her origins, the chastity in her heart, her courage in battle, her love for the land of France, but above all, the holiness in her life and death," said Bishop Felix Dupanloup. He was speaking on May 8, 1869, at the annual festival in Orléans honoring Jeanne d'Arc for liberating that city on the same day in 1429. He further remarked: "Do not think you must choose between the duties of a Christian and those of a Frenchman. Religion points its finger toward the sky, but it does not make us forget our poor country down here."[165]

Bishop Dupanloup went to each of the diocesan bishops of the territories through which Joan the Maid had traveled to enlist their support with him and the people of Orléans in presenting Joan's cause to the Holy See.[166] Documenting Joan's widespread appeal among the people and hierarchy of France and beyond, Bishop (later Cardinal) Dupanloup of Orléans (1846–1878) initiated the official canonical proceedings toward sainthood for Joan of Arc.

Undoubtedly the political, social, and religious tumult in France, Europe, and the Church during the previous four and a half centuries since Joan's death contributed to the very long delay by the Catholic Church in judging her cause. Although

---

[165] Wilson-Smith, *Joan of Arc: Maid, Myth and History*, 183.
[166] Pernoud and Clin, *Joan of Arc: Her Story*, 245.

popular support for Joan of Arc remained strong throughout France, the Franco-Prussian War and the frenzy of nationalism in Italy, which resulted in the loss of the Papal States, preoccupied the Holy See, making Pope Pius IX a literal prisoner of the Vatican. In 1874 Joan's case resumed. All documents and testimonials involving the condemnation, relapse, and rehabilitation trials were translated from medieval French and Latin and then examined.

The process of declaring someone to be a saint of the Catholic Church (canonization) has undergone considerable development over the centuries. For the first millennium of Christianity, martyrdom or public renown for great holiness was the only requirement for special burial in a crypt or chapel, where spontaneous popular devotion flourished. A small town could revere its local "saint" who might not be widely known beyond the region until the reputation and heavenly influence of that soul became manifest elsewhere. The voice of the people was the voice of God. Eventually the bishop of a territory might approve and encourage the people's pious devotion to that holy person.

On his own authority and at his own discretion, though, the Roman pontiff could set or suspend the standards and modify the procedures for the causes of saints. He also could universalize devotion to those souls by establishing their feast days in the general (worldwide) liturgical calendar of the Latin Church or simply leave those liturgical celebrations at the national level. The first recorded pontifical canonization was on January 31, 998, when Pope John XVI, at a conclave of his cardinals, officially declared Ulrich of Augsburg to be a saint of God and of the Latin Church.[167] During the second Christian millennium,

---

[167] Tavard, *The Spiritual Way of St. Jeanne d'Arc*, 71.

popes and local bishops with their Church officials set more formal standards of investigation before publicly declaring the sanctity of candidate souls and proposing them for public veneration in churches.

Always the first and foremost standard to be met was verification of a candidate's virtues, especially of faith, hope, and charity. The advocate for a holy candidate was called the defender, known now as the postulator, who had to overcome all possible objections from the promoter of the Faith, then commonly known as the devil's advocate. The promoter searched for any vice or serious fault in the candidate's life and death to accuse that soul and thwart the advancement of the cause. The second standard was a high intensity and wide extent of popular devotion for the cause of that soul. The third standard was the certification of miracles involving bodily healings from God through that holy person's intercession in heaven. In the canonical causes for martyrs of Christian Faith, the Church dispensed from the normal requirement for miracles. At the end of the nineteenth century and the start of the twentieth, the advocating defender of the candidate had to document four miracles in the canonization process.

Jehanne La Pucelle was a defendant in a total of six ecclesiastical trials: four while she was alive and two after her death. The first two verdicts favored her: at Toul, when the bishop recognized her private vow of virginity that nullified her suitor's claim of marriage, and at Poitiers, when a panel of prelates and clerics endorsed her character and her mission on behalf of Charles VII. In occupied Rouen the long third trial condemned her and the fourth, a short sequel trial, judged her guilty of relapse, which guaranteed her death by fire. The fifth time her case went to ecclesiastical court was in liberated Rouen, with depositions also taken at Paris, during the rehabilitation or nullification trial, which concluded twenty-five years after her death. The last trial, begun at Orléans and ended in Rome, took the Church more than fifty years to reach a final verdict in judgment of Joan of Arc, nearly five centuries after her death.[168] The investigation, or inquisition, that opened in Orléans after the Franco-Prussian War consisted of thirty-three sessions, lasting a little more than one year. Two more inquisitions under Bishop Coullie, Bishop Dupanloup's successor, totaled fifty-eight sessions over several years and concluded in 1888. The case then went to a tribunal of the Sacred Congregation of Rites at the Holy See. In 1892 under the pontificate of Pope Leo XIII, the earliest Roman phase began to consider the reputation for sanctity of Joan of Arc.[169]

Joan's defender in Rome was Hilary Alibrandi. Her opponent there was the promoter Augustine Caprara. Caprara began his case against Joan by acknowledging her initially heroic virtues and then concluded his opening remarks by her documented lapse: "It seems then that two stages are to be discerned in the life of our Maid. The first was glorious and full of admiration, up to her captivity.... But when she was captured and subject to judicial questions, that greatness of soul gave out, that splendor of divine revelations vanished, and grave faults are seen to have obscured the aforesaid virtues, whatever, finally, they were."[170] The devil's advocate had begun again to seed those doubts!

The Sacred Congregation of Rites in 1892 was also considering the case of Christopher Columbus, whose zeal for propagating

---

[168] Henry Ansgar Kelly, "Joan of Arc's Last Trial: The Attack of the Devil's Advocates," in *Fresh Verdicts on Joan of Arc*, 205.
[169] Kelly, "Joan of Arc's Last Trial," 206.
[170] Ibid., 207.

the Christian Faith in the Americas was widely recognized. Of him and others Pope Leo XIII had written that "the signs of divine power also appear in those [who] shine forth a certain excellent forcefulness of spirit and mind." Joan's devotees and her defender pressed ahead in their determination to demonstrate the heroic forcefulness of her soul, imbued with supernatural virtue along with those natural moral virtues characteristic of her life and death.

Alibrandi introduced many testimonials from bishops and other notable clergymen and laymen postulating Joan's heroic virtues, but these remained unanswered by Caprara or were dismissed as not indicative of the miraculous. Regarding Joan's reputation, the promoter Caprara considered her to be admired for military prowess, not for Christian virtue, that she had not wide acclaim for heroic virtue at her rehabilitation trial.[171]

The third standard to be met was a consideration of martyrdom, as her defender and other proponents advocated. The promoter, however, while admitting Joan's reputation as perhaps a martyr of modesty or a martyr for her individual faith in God, countered that dying for one's private revelation cannot be called martyrdom for the Faith in witness to the public revelation of God in Scripture and Tradition. Besides, he said, Joan's devotees could not prove any miracles from God through her intercession. Caprara concluded his case by considering obstacles to the pontifical court's approval of Joan's cause, which could bring discredit to the Church for having condemned her in the 1431 trial at which so many notable clerics and theologians were present.[172] He used "political correctness" to excuse and shield

---

[171] Ibid., 208–209.
[172] Ibid., 210–213.

corrupt churchmen before him from shame, about a century before the term was even invented.

Promoter Caprara apparently regretted his role in having to present 54 pages of adversarial commentary along with 47 pages of documents in opposition to the Maid. Yet, admitting to her spiritual importance within France, his summation also noted her supranational significance. Her acclaimed heroic sanctity by the peoples of Europe also extended far into the Americas. Joan of Arc's defender, Alibrandi, had presented 170 pages of strong, well-documented testimony, which postulated her virtuous life and death. After a vote in her favor by an assembly of his cardinals and noting the reprehensible trial in 1431 by clergy proponents of the invalid and schismatic Council of Basel, Pope Leo XIII on January 27, 1894, signed a decree for the cause of the Venerable Servant of God Joan of Arc, virgin (*Causae Ven. Servae Dei Ioannae de Arc, Virginis*).[173]

Step 1 was completed by that papal decree of Venerable Joan. The Church began step 2 with a new defender, Xavier Hertzog, and another promoter, John Baptist Lugari. "Is there certainty regarding the theological virtues of faith, hope, and charity toward God and neighbor and also concerning the cardinal virtues of prudence, justice, fortitude, and temperance, and associated virtues, to a heroic degree, in the matter and to the effect that is being investigated?" Negative, concluded Lugari, who took the same line of reasoning as his predecessor but went so far as to question the pope and cardinals' previous decision in declaring Joan Venerable! Lugari said that Joan had relied on her own judgment in the matter of her private revelations rather than submitting to the Church's authority and judgment.

[173] Kelly, "Joan of Arc's Last Trial," 214–215.

Nevertheless, after the consulters evaluated also the impressive number of favorable documents introduced in the preliminaries of 1898, a majority of them decided that "the difficulties of the Promoter of the Faith have been satisfactorily resolved." Those proceedings, published in 1901 with a favorable decision, meant that the next two phases could commence in the process toward beatification.[174]

Yet a third promoter of the Faith, Alexander Verde, began his own series of devilish attacks on the Maid's cause by attempting to discredit her favorable witnesses for their lack of strong documentary evidence: "For the juridical inquests are encrusted with the five centuries elapsed since the actions occurred, and therefore the witnesses clearly rely on documents and histories; for which reason they do not even seem to deserve the name of witnesses." The promoter Verde went further in deriding defender John Baptist Minetti's case by suggesting his modern sources relied on newspaper accounts and stage plays to establish Joan's virtues! Verde was obviously aware of the growing worldwide fascination with the amazing Maid since 1869, when Bishop Dupanloup first publicized her holy cause. Joan's fame was international by the turn of the twentieth century, not only among Catholics, such as the great nineteenth-century Italian composer and patriot Giuseppe Verdi, who wrote one of his many dramatic operas on Giovanna d'Arco, but even among non-Catholics. The Russian musician Peter Ilyich Tchaikovsky, for instance, composed a fanciful opera about her; the popular American humorist Mark Twain wrote about her; and the well-known English playwright George Bernard Shaw composed a play around her character. Moreover, French and Italian pioneer

---

[174] Ibid., 216–219.

filmmakers as early as 1897, 1898, and 1901 were producing short movies featuring the Maid. The devil's advocate Verde discounted all the popular sentiment and proceeded to suggest that perhaps all of Joan of Arc's voices were manifestations of hysteria.[175]

John Baptist Minetti, on defender Herzog's team of advocates, became the principal adversary to the devil's advocate Verde. Minetti derided Verde's insinuations of hysteria using quotations from the previous promoters, Caprara and Lugari, which admitted Joan's voices of probable divine origin. Minetti's documented summation evidently overcame most doubts, such that the consulters in Joan's case voted favorably to send their conclusions to the pope for a meeting with his cardinals and all the consulters. At that meeting in November 1903, after the cardinals and the consulters had voted, the new pope, Pius X, postponed his decision, asking the assembly to pray for his correct discernment of God's will in such a difficult matter. On the solemnity of the Epiphany of the Lord, January 6, 1904, Pope Pius X sent Joan of Arc a little birthday present, saying she had truly lived the virtues in a heroic degree and her cause could proceed to the next phase, the discussion of miracles. Three were approved; and in a unanimous vote of the assembly in April 1909, Pope Pius X named her Blessed Joan of Arc.

A few years after Joan's beatification, Europe's Great War began. Brokenhearted and distressed at the inevitable carnage among his "children," the saintly Pope Pius X died. After that "war to end all wars," the "canonization trial" of Joan of Arc resumed. The Congregation for Rites certified the fourth miracle required in those years and concluded the last trial of the Maid.

[175] Kelly, "Joan of Arc's Last Trial," 221, 225–228.

The Church Militant finally recognized what the Church Triumphant had known for nearly five hundred years. On May 16, 1920, the Roman pontiff Benedict XV, surrounded by thousands of devotees assembled in the Vatican Basilica of Saint Peter, declared Jeanne d'Arc to be *Saint* Joan of Arc!

> *Let us give thanks to the Father for having made you worthy to share the lot of the saints in light. He rescued us from the power of darkness and brought us into the kingdom of His beloved Son. Through Him we have redemption, the forgiveness of our sins.* (cf. Col. 1:12–14, NAB)

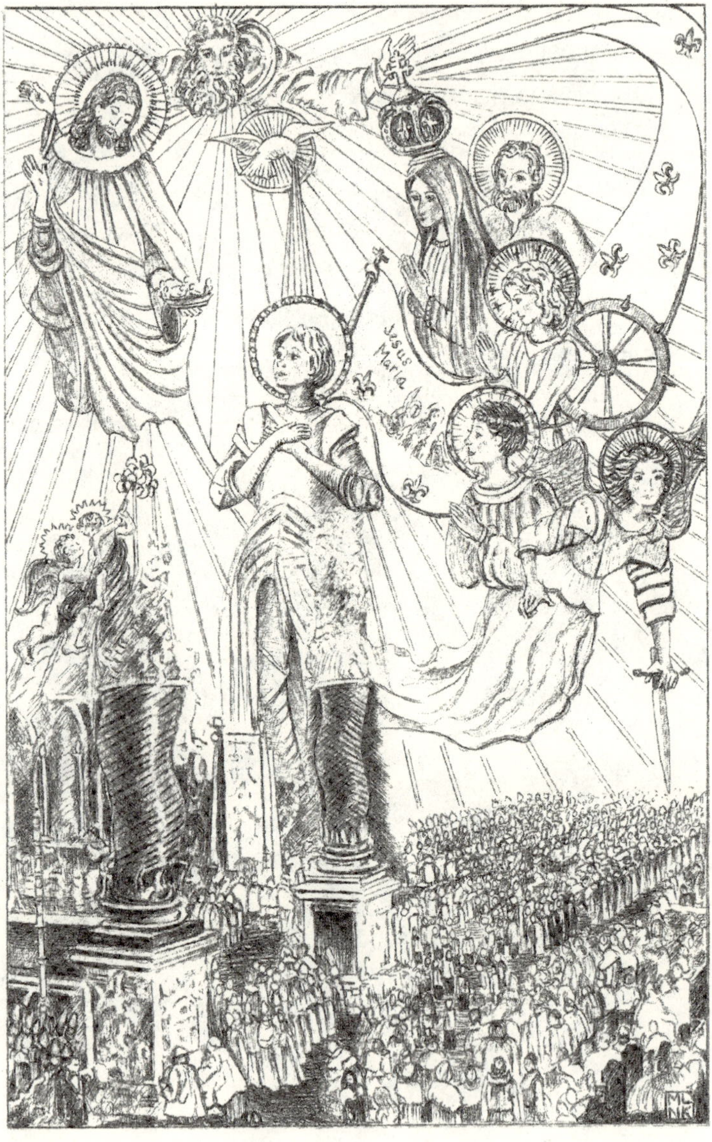
Jesus
Maria

✠ Meditation ✠

TRANSFORMATION BY GRACE

"Why are there strife and passion, schisms and even war among you? Do we not possess the same Spirit of grace which was given to us and the same calling in Christ? Why do we tear apart and divide the Body of Christ? We should put an end to this division immediately. Let us fall down before our Master and implore His mercy with our tears. Then He will be reconciled to us and restore us to the practice of brotherly love that befits us." Thus Pope Saint Clement, third successor to Saint Peter as bishop of Rome, expressed his anguish in a letter to the Corinthians, admonishing them for their disunity, as Saint Paul had done in his inspired letters to them forty years before. Three centuries later, Bishop Saint Gregory of Nyssa in Asia Minor gave a similar exhortation to the Church: "If by a diligent life of virtue you wash away the film of dirt that covers your heart, then the divine Beauty will shine forth in you."[176]

Historians record the evidence of recurring warfare and hostility among families, peoples, and nations since the beginning and throughout the millennia of human beings on this earth. Both Hebrew and Christian Scriptures and Church histories have documented many periods of controversy, contention, and conflict even among the people of God. "Do you think that I have come to bring peace on earth? No, I tell you, but rather division!" (Luke 12:51). Those sobering words of the Lord Jesus confirm the divine intention to engage in war against evil, to

---

[176] *Liturgy of the Hours*, Office of Readings.

divide families and communities and nations from their evil ways, and to win the victory over sin and death and hell itself. The Apostle to the Gentiles reminds believers to persevere in their hope for individual and communal victory during their spiritual combat: "For we are not contending against flesh and blood, but against the principalities, against the powers, against the world rulers of this present darkness" (Eph. 6:12). With that insight and understanding, the Church has always taught the powerful, beautiful way of virtue and truth, even when Christians have not always practiced faithfully and charitably the divine doctrine. Vices mar the beauty of God's image in human beings. In every epoch of salvation history, each person and all communities need repentance, reconciliation, and renewal. The "pitiable state" of the Church in early, medieval, and modern times, in France, in Europe, and around the globe, has always needed reformation and transformation by divine graces and mercies.

"It is a matter of coming to an interior reconciliation in the heart of the Church. Looking back over the past, to the divisions which in the course of the centuries have rent the Body of Christ, one continually has the impression that, at critical moments when divisions were coming about, not enough was done by the Church's leaders to maintain or regain reconciliation and unity." Pope Benedict XVI admitted that failure to his fellow bishops in 2007, when issuing his apostolic letter *Summorum Pontificum*, which clarified the traditional and modern forms of worship in the Roman Missal of the Catholic Church. His critique is perfectly applicable to the situation of the Church in the fifteenth century, as also in the centuries before and since then until today. It is also a matter of coming to an interior recognition in the mind of the Church hierarchy that many clergy have not reflected the virtues of the Good Shepherd in their own lives, actions, and judgments toward the laity. In fact, some of them have instead displayed the worst vices.

The judges at Rouen showed their arrogance when they maligned and disparaged the humble, unschooled peasant Maiden. Their unveiled contempt for her was obvious in the distortion of the term *Church Militant* to mean only themselves, when that expression includes all Christians in the world, laity with clergy, who are engaged in spiritual warfare against the Enemy of souls. Even when those Rouen bishops invoked their divine teaching authority, their Magisterium, to gain Joan's assent of faith and obedience to them exclusively as the Church Militant, they did so apart from the pope, to whom Joan had appealed. Bishop Cauchon had developed the idea of a dual monarchy for the English; he furthermore supported the schismatic Council of Basel against papal authority. His refusal to send Joan's appeal to the pope was tantamount to a dual magisterium. Cauchon and his arrogant academicians from the University of Paris were more than five centuries ahead of today's modernist heretics who consider priest-"theologians" as equals of the Catholic pope and bishops.

Church leaders have not always avoided politicizing the gospel or reducing its content to social and economic benefits for themselves or their own nations. Only by the imitation of Christ, our faithful and compassionate High Priest, can Christian clergymen foster this interior reconciliation with God and unity within the universal Church among families, communities, and nations. The gospel proclamation certainly has positive transforming effects on society, but only when individual Christians, their families, and their religious leaders demonstrate holy faith by virtuous lives and charitable deeds. Christ Jesus taught the truth of God and revealed the Father of mercies, the God of all consolation (cf. 2 Cor. 1:3), by His good deeds, especially by

His consummate act of love on His holy Cross. So too, when Christians truly exemplify Christ by their morally upright Christian lives and charitable works of mercy, nonbelievers become convinced of the authenticity of the gospel message, and they cooperate with God the Holy Spirit in the reformation and transformation of their lives and societies.

The biggest obstacle to a soul's development in the spiritual life is the sin of pride, which puts one's self in the place of God and refuses to act like God. Pride is the refusal "to love what God loves," as the imprisoned Joan of Arc beautifully expressed to her condemnation trial judges. Humility, by contrast, is the most important virtue for rapid advancement in the spiritual life of divine grace. From a very early age, Jeannette of Domrémy realized who she was and what dignity she possessed. She prayed daily, which showed she was dependent on God and grateful to Him for the good family of her birth and the honorable townsfolk in her community. She recognized God's voice through His heavenly emissaries identifying her as "virgin" and "daughter of God." From Almighty God she humbly received a great commission, as a soldier of Christ leading fellow Christian soldiers, to liberate her country and reunite the nation under God, for the good of her people and herself.

Joan had made that private vow of virginity at age thirteen and reaffirmed it publicly at age sixteen, when she refused the marriage contract to which she had never given her consent. Her modesty and chastity were repeatedly noted by her male soldier companions. Furthermore, her leadership in virtue resulted in her soldiers' imitation of her virtues, their inspiration and the resultant liberation of the French people from the English invaders, and the renewal of the nation of France. Her vindicated life and Christlike death left a beautiful example for the Church of

God throughout Europe and the world. Living and dying amid the Hundred Years' War, beatified and canonized around World War I, Joan of Arc deserves the title of martyr, along with that of virgin. "Joan of Arc still matters, since in her story Church and country, myth and history intersect."[177] "It is natural ... to honor one who sought no crown or glory, whose life was given to the cause in as painful, pitiful a manner as any martyr. Let us remember her in reverence, study her story, learn the lesson of that life, and honor her as a hero; for in so doing the inspiration comes to every individual, ennobling and elevating."[178]

---

[177] Wilson-Smith, *Joan of Arc: Maid, Myth and History*, 225.
[178] 1913 Committee in *Joan of Arc Exhibition Catalogue*, 8.

Conclusion

*Great and wonderful are thy deeds, O Lord God Almighty.
Just and true are thy ways, O King of the ages. . . . For thou
alone art holy. All the nations shall come and worship thee.*

—Revelation 15:3–4

*Then I saw a great white throne and him who sat upon it . . .
and I heard a great voice from the throne saying,
"Behold, the dwelling of God is with men. He will dwell
with them, and they shall be his people, and
God himself will be with them [as their God]."*

—Revelation 20:11; 21:3

⚜

Sainte Jeanne d'Arc, the religious patriot and citizen-saint, patroness of France, has become a powerful friend, advocate, and spiritual sister for millions of men and women around the world, soldiers and civilians alike. Although having had an unrepeatable, unique vocation from God, she endures as an inspiring model for those who have dedicated their lives to noble pursuits and have followed Christ in God's universal call to holiness. During the six centuries since her birth, countless young women and men have entered the consecrated, religious life because of her stellar witness of virginity, fidelity to the will of God the Father, and love for Jesus and Mary and the saints of God.

> *With the God of armies giving you victory,*
> *You drove out the stranger and had the king anointed.*
> *But this was still only an ephemeral glory.*
> *Your name was due the halo of the Saints.*
>
> *Deep in a black cell, burdened with heavy chains,*
> *The cruel stranger heaped sorrows upon you.*
> *In your dark prison you appear to me more beautiful*
> *Than at the coronation of your king.*

That celestial gleam of eternal glory,
Who brought it to you? That was betrayal.

—Thérèse Martin (May 1897)

Thérèse Martin (1873–1897), who had made her first Holy Communion at the unusually young age of six years, also received an exceptional papal dispensation to enter the cloistered Carmelite convent of Lisieux, France, at the age of sixteen. Inspired throughout her short life by La Pucelle, Thérèse likened her own "little way" of humility in the love of God and her year-long suffering from tuberculosis to the saintly Jeanne d'Arc's year-long imprisonment and her death, as a kind of spiritual martyrdom.

Saint Thérèse of the Child Jesus, popularly called the Little Flower, was canonized in 1925—only five years after Saint Joan's canonization—and was, by another papal decree, declared a Doctor of the Church in 1997, having also exerted an enormous influence on the spirituality of millions of Christians around the world. Undoubtedly Saint Joan was interceding with the Holy Spirit for Thérèse's rapid development in wisdom and sanctifying grace from her childhood, as well as for her speedy canonization after death. What a contrast with the ponderously slow process of the Church Militant that took nearly five centuries to acknowledge Saint Joan's heroic virtues and venerate her at God's altars!

Saint Joan of Arc has inspired many thousands of poems, essays, books, artworks, plays, films, musical compositions, college study programs, and even Internet websites. "I studied that girl, Joan of Arc, for twelve years, and it never seemed to me that the artists and the writers gave us a true picture of her. They drew a picture of a peasant. Her dress was that of a peasant. But they always missed the face—the divine soul, the pure character, the supreme woman, the wonderful girl," exclaimed Mark Twain about his favorite historical personage, when he spoke at a dinner for magazine and newspaper artists and illustrators in New York City in 1905.[179] "Joan's life, to meet the demands of art, is organized by dramatists and by historians and biographers with a dramatic sense.... Her story is always intended to exhort and to indoctrinate others to revere her high example. She is a heroine in the sphere of moral action; in literature, she does not inspire precautionary pity and fear, but incites us to imitation."[180]

Many Catholic parish churches in the United States—and maybe even a few Anglican or Episcopalian communities—bear the name of Saint Joan of Arc as their patron saint. A far greater number of churches, such as the Catholic chapel at West Point, have within them at least one fine artistic image of the soldier-saint in a stained-glass window, a painting, or a statue. Outdoors in a main plaza within the French Quarter in New Orleans, Louisiana, a massive, imposing statue of the triumphant Maid mounted on horseback inspires awe and admiration in the viewers beneath it.

Even in the homeland of her former enemies, another statue of Joan of Arc, rendered in shining armor with upright sword in her right hand, was erected in 1923 inside England's Winchester Cathedral by that Anglican diocese. Dedicated as a mark of reparation at that time to the recently canonized Catholic saint, her statue stands directly opposite the tomb of

---

[179] Mark Twain quoted in a *New York Times* article of December 31, 1905.
[180] Fraioli, *Joan of Arc and the Hundred Years War*, 169.

Cardinal Henry Beaufort, the English churchman who had co-presided with Bishop Pierre Cauchon at Joan's condemnation trial.[181] At least Joan received some artistic and poetic justice from the English!

Yet outside the village of her birth and in the old city marketplace of her death stand the two most significant churches that enshrine the marvelous story of the Maid of Lorraine. Near her rustic native village of Domrémy, about a kilometer from her childhood home, next to the small medieval chapel where Joan was baptized, stands a majestic Gothic shrine church overlooking the peaceful, bucolic valley below it. That very site was once the location of the Bois Chenu, the ancient woods with the Fairy Tree, or Lady Tree, where Joan gathered beautiful flowers to honor the Blessed Mother of God. Outside the shrine church are four finely sculptured and newly gilded statues, which represent the young Joan kneeling to receive God's call from Saint Michael the Archangel, along with Saints Catherine and Margaret, virgin martyrs of ancient Christian times. Inside the shrine crypt chapel is the very same statue of Our Lady of Bermont that the girl Jeannette venerated. On the upper church walls are several beautiful murals portraying scenes in the life of Joan, among them her first Holy Communion, her heroic leadership of soldiers arrayed in battle, her noble presence at her king's coronation, her burning at the stake, and her final spiritual triumph among the saints in heaven.

In the city of Rouen, where Joan was harshly imprisoned, then unjustly and maliciously tried by a politicized Church tribunal, a stark, modernistic shrine church now stands over the very spot in the old marketplace where the English and their

---

[181] Ó'Floinn, *Three French Saints: The One Who Led an Army*, 112.

CONCLUSION

colluding Burgundians scornfully mocked and brutally burned her at the stake, calling her a relapsed heretic, apostate, blasphemer, and sorceress. Within that sacred place made holy by her fiery death in witness to Christ, the Church now welcomes multitudes of devoted pilgrims every year. My American friends and I were among them on April 30, 2012, near the end of our pilgrimage honoring Saint Joan's sixth centennial. We had previously visited Domrémy, Orléans, and Reims before celebrating Holy Mass in Rouen.

Elsewhere around the Christian world, thousands of churches and shrines draw more than a billion faithful people to worship God, the Most Holy Trinity; to give homage to our Lord Jesus Christ, King of kings, and to our Lady, Mary Immaculate, Queen of the Universe; and to honor the saints of God. Among that vast throng of holy persons within the Church Triumphant in heaven, already ennobled and meritoriously crowned by the hands of Christ the High Priest and True Bishop of all souls, is the virgin daughter of God and of Holy Mother Church, Princess Joan. Baptized in the holy water and confirmed in the divine fire of the Holy Spirit, she drank first of the precious Blood Royal of King Jesus in his eucharistic Sacrament and then of her own Christian chalice of suffering and death in witness to Him. As the Passion of the Christ and the Passion of the Maid were commingled on earth, so too are the kingdom, the power, and the glory of Jesus and Joan united in heaven by the one divine Love.

For us within the Church Militant on earth, still heavily engaged in the holy war against the evil Enemy of souls, our Lady Joan radiantly and powerfully continues her witness by the Holy Spirit as a virtuous, victorious virgin martyr with Christ Jesus. He is the Victim Lamb once slain, who lives forever as our joyful hope for mercy, justice, and peace. "And He shall reign for ever and ever, King of kings and Lord of lords! Halleluia!"

Father Michael Joseph Cerrone III
January 6, 2015
603rd anniversary of the birth of Saint Joan of Arc

Prayers

✠

PRAYER FOR SAINT JOAN OF ARC'S INTERCESSION

O Lord our God, who chose the Virgin of Domrémy, Saint Joan of Arc, for the defense of the Faith and the Fatherland, we beseech you by her intercession to grant us peace among the nations as well as peace in our souls. We ask you this by virtue of the merits of Jesus Christ our Lord.[182]

---

[182] Published by the priests of Saint Rémy Church, the place of Saint Joan's Baptism in Domrémy, France.

Litany of Saint Joan Of Arc
(Feast day on May 30)

Lord, have mercy. *Christ, have mercy.*
Lord, have mercy; Christ, hear us. *Christ, graciously hear us.*
God the Father of heaven, *have mercy on us.*
God the Son, Redeemer of the world, *have mercy on us.*
God the Holy Spirit, the Paraclete, *have mercy on us.*
Holy Trinity, one God, *have mercy on us.*
Holy Mary, Virgin Mother of God, *pray for us.*
Our Lady of Prompt Succor, *pray for us.*
Saint Michael the Archangel, *pray for us.*
Saint Gabriel the Archangel, *pray for us.*
Saint Raphael the Archangel, *pray for us.*
All great and holy angels given us by God, *pray for us.*
Saint Joan of Arc:
    Chosen by God, *pray for us.*
    Informed of your mission by Saint Michael, *pray for us.*
    Compliant to the call of God, *pray for us.*
    Confiding in and submissive to your Voices, *pray for us.*
    Model of family life and labor, *pray for us.*
    Faithfully devoted to our Lady, *pray for us.*
    Delighting in the Holy Eucharist, *pray for us.*
    Model of generosity in service of God, *pray for us.*
    Example of fidelity to the divine vocation, *pray for us.*
    Model of union with God in action, *pray for us.*

Virgin and soldier, *pray for us.*
Model of courage and purity in the field of battle,
    pray for us.
Compassionate toward all who suffer, *pray for us.*
Pride of Orléans, *pray for us.*
Glory of Reims, *pray for us.*
Liberator of France, *pray for us.*
Abandoned and imprisoned at Compiègne, *pray
    for us.*
Pure and patient prisoner, *pray for us.*
Heroic and valiant before your judges, *pray for us.*
Alone with God at your hour of torment, *pray for us.*
Martyr of Rouen, *pray for us.*
Saint Joan of Arc and Saint Thérèse of Lisieux, patronesses of France, *intercede for us.*
Saint Louis, King of France, *intercede for us.*
All saints of France, *intercede for us.*

FOR GOD AND COUNTRY

⚜

The Epiphany of Jesus and Joan[183]

A bright superstar shines its radiant light:
The Star of David shows the Way, the Truth, the Life —
The Epiphany of the Lord has dawned.

The Son of God, Jesus the Christ,
In wondrous birth at Bethlehem,
Gives hope to a nation, Israel oppressed,
With promised hope for the world,
For those who believe in the God of love,
For those who are distressed.
Grace and peace, justice and mercy now shown;
God's goodness, kindness, and tender compassion are
    known.

Fourteen centuries and twelve years later,
On another Epiphany Day,
That heavenly Star once again shone bright
Over the frontier town of Domrémy,
That the people be freed from their miserable plight.
Born and baptized of pious patriots,
A daughter of God was Joan of Arc, by name.
Her destiny was to save her country
From its pitiable state, from its public shame.

With absolute trust in her mission from God
And her devotion to Jesus and Mary,
Joan, called Jeannette by family and friends,

[183] Copyright © 2010 by Michael J. Cerrone III.

Left home and was led by an archangel
    and saints.
"Go, daughter of God!" exhorted her Voices:
Liberate your people from the enemy invader;
Unite your nation under the Almighty Redeemer;
Hail Christ, King of kings, as Victorious Ruler!

A holy warrior was Jeanne La Pucelle, the virgin
    soldier of God.
Like Christ, Lord of armies, she sought justice
    with honor:
"The soldiers will fight and God will bring
    victory!"
First and foremost, among her generals and
    troops,
Joan commanded virtue and ended vice.
They confessed their sins before each battle.
They followed her in prayer, penance, and
    holy Sacrifice:
They became loyal to the Precious Blood Royal.

Her attempts at peace and dire warnings unheeded,
A bold armed force against the enemy was needed.
She rallied her men by courage, not might;
Even when wounded she returned to the fight.
Her leadership was unquestioned, her compassion
    unmatched.
As Jesus wept over Jerusalem, which languished,
Joan too wept over the fallen, even the enemy
    vanquished.

Then, after defeating the siege of a city renowned,
Joan's army marched on to see her king anointed and
 crowned.
On earth she would never again witness victory,
Only disloyalty, deceit, and vile treachery.
Her heavenly Voices spoke of capture and martyrdom,
Not the consolation of fame in a worldly kingdom.

The Passion Play has now unfolded, for Jesus and for
 Joan—
His arrest and suffering was the pattern for her own.
Unjust trials and wicked high priests, Caiaphas then
 Cauchon,
In envy and with avarice used politics over religion—
One to appease a Roman governor, the bishop an
 English regent.

The Sacrifice on the Cross by Christ is the Father's
 mercy revealed.
The Sacred Heart of Jesus' wounds, in Body and in
 Soul,
Become the source of man's salvation, that sinners can
 be healed.
The sacrifice on the stake by Joan, her body in the fire,
Shows that nothing evil can ever destroy a pure-hearted
 love's desire:
"Jesus! Jesus! Jesus!" Joan cried aloud, and expired.

"Truly this was the Son of God!" proclaimed the Roman
 soldier with the lance.
"God, have mercy; I burned a saint!" exclaimed the
 English soldier with the torch.

Jesus alone kindles the fire of the Holy Spirit's love:
Joan's soul is now aflame in Him among the saints
 above.
How long it took the Church in Rome to praise the
 noble life of Joan!
How many souls she still inspires to overcome their
 base desires,
To live in virtue with goodwill for all humanity,
That every nation on this earth would worship God
 the Almighty!

Jesus, Prince of Peace, now reigns, and with Him
 Princess Joan.
On them and on the saints above are merited crowns
 of gold.
God calls us all to follow, the Cross before the Crown,
Our Good Shepherd gathering His sheep into one fold.
Let us enlist ourselves with zeal in this cause of Christ,
To march together as one Church and never stray
 alone,
That we may share eternity in God's glory manifest—
In the radiant Epiphany of Jesus and Joan.

Bibliography

"Joan of Arc's First Letter to the English at Orléans," March 22, 1429. Translated by Allen Williamson. Joan of Arc Archive. http://www.archive.joan-of-arc.org/joanofarc_letter_Mar1429.html.

American Numismatic Society. *Joan of Arc Loan Exhibition Catalogue.* 1913 exhibit in New York City.

Astell, Ann W., and Bonnie Wheeler, eds. *Joan of Arc and Spirituality.* New York: Macmillan, 2003.

Banfield, Susan. *Joan of Arc.* New York: Chelsea House Publishers, 1988.

Bartlett, J. V. *The Popes: A Papal History.* Scottsdale, AZ: SimRidge Publishing, 1990.

Beevers, John. *Saint Joan of Arc.* Rockford, IL: TAN Books, 1974.

Benedict XVI. "On Joan of Arc." Wednesday audience, January 26, 2011, Rome. Translated by Zenit News Agency.

———. *Caritas in Veritate* (*Charity in Truth*). Encyclical letter. June 29, 2009. http://www.vatican.va/holy_father/benedict_xvi/encyclicals/documents/hf_ben-xvi_enc_20090629_caritas-in-veritate_en.html.

Buchan, Alice. *Joan of Arc and the Recovery of France*. Edited by A. L. Rouse. New York: Macmillan, 1948.

Bunson, Matthew. *Encyclopedia of Catholic History*. Huntington, IN: Our Sunday Visitor, 1995.

Cameron, Peter John, ed. *Benedictus: Day by Day with Pope Benedict XVI*. San Francisco: Ignatius Press/Magnificat, 2006.

Catholic Encyclopedia. New York: Robert Appleton Company, 1910.

Chaput, Archbishop Charles. "On Military Service." Lecture given at the U.S. Air Force Academy, Colorado Springs, Colorado, October 25, 2010.

Chullikatt, Archbishop Francis. "The Nuclear Question: The Church's Teachings and the Current State of Affairs." Address given in Kansas City, Missouri, on July 23, 2011. Zenit. http://www.zenit.org/en/articles/archbishop-chullikatt-s-address-on-the-nuclear-question.

Cohen, William A. *Wisdom of the Generals*. Paramus, NJ: Prentice Hall Press, 2001.

DeVries, Kelly. *Joan of Arc: A Military Leader*. Stroud: Sutton, 1999.

Fraioli, Deborah A. *Joan of Arc and the Hundred Years War*. Westport, CT: Greenwood Press, 2005.

BIBLIOGRAPHY

Gies, Frances. *Joan of Arc: the Legend and the Reality*. New York: Harper-Row Publishers, 1981.

Girault, Pierre-Gilles. *Joan of Arc*. Translated by Angela Caldwell. Éditions Jean-Paul Gisserot, 2004.

Goldstone, Nancy. *The Maid and the Queen: The Secret History of Joan of Arc*. New York: Viking, 2012.

Gondoin, Stéphane William. *The Siege of Orléans and the Loire Campaign, 1428–1429: Joan of Arc and the Passage to Victory*. Translated by Jennifer Meyniel. Paris: Histoire and Collections, 2010.

Gonzalez, Justo L. *The Story of Christianity*. New York: Harper-Collins, 1984, 1985.

Gordon, Mary. *Joan of Arc*. New York: Lipper/Viking, 2000.

Hopkins, Andrea. *Six Medieval Women*. New York: Barnes and Noble, 1997.

International Committee on English in the Liturgy. *Liturgy of the Hours*. New York: Catholic Book Publishing, 1975. Psalms from *The Grail*. London: Collins, 1973.

Lang, Andrew. *The Maid of France*. London: Longmans, Green, 1909.

Nash-Marshall, Siobhan. *Joan of Arc: A Spiritual Biography*. New York: Crossroad, 1999.

Ó'Floinn, Críostóir. *Joan of Arc: The One Who Led an Army*. Dublin: Columba Press, 2009.

Pernoud, Régine, and Marie-Veronique Clin. *Joan of Arc: Her Story*. Translated by Jeremy duQuesnay Adams. New York: St. Martin's Press, 1968.

Pernoud, Régine. *Joan of Arc: By Herself and Her Witnesses.* Translated by Edward Hyams. New York: Stein and Day, 1966.

———. *The Retrial of Joan of Arc.* Translated by J. M. Cohen. San Francisco: Ignatius Press, 2007.

Pius XII. *Society and Politics.* A collection of writings and addresses by Pope Pius XII on various subjects, published by the Holy See. From a copy owned by Sr. Margherita Marchione, M.R.F.

Richey, Stephen W. *Joan of Arc: The Warrior Saint.* Westport, CT: Praeger, 2003.

Robo, Etienne. *Saint Joan: The Woman and the Saint.* New York: Spiritual Book Associates, 1947, 1948.

Russell, Preston. *Lights of Madness: In Search of Joan of Arc.* Savannah: Frederic C. Beil, 2005.

Sackville-West, Victoria. *Saint Joan of Arc.* Garden City, NY: Country Life Press, 1936.

Shaw, Russell, ed. *Encyclopedia of Catholic Doctrine.* Huntington, IN: Our Sunday Visitor Publishing, 1997.

Spoto, Donald. *Joan: The Mysterious Life of the Heretic Who Became a Saint.* New York: HarperCollins, 2007.

Stolpe, Sven. *The Maid of Orléans.* Translated by Eric Lewenhaupt. New York: Pantheon, 1956.

Tavard, George H. *The Spiritual Way of Ste. Jeanne d'Arc.* Collegeville, MN: Liturgical Press, 1998.

The Trial of Jeanne D'Arc. The official record translated by W. P. Barrett. New York: Gotham House, 1932.

Twain, Mark. *Joan of Arc.* San Francisco: Ignatius Press, 1989.

Warner, Marina. *Joan of Arc: The Image of Female Heroism*. New York: Alfred A. Knopf, 1981.

Wheeler, Bonnie, and Charles T. Wood, eds. *Fresh Verdicts on Joan of Arc*. New York: Garland Publishing, 1996.

Wheeler, Bonnie. Medieval Heroines in History and Legend (Part II). Great Courses lecture series on CD. Chantilly, VA: Teaching Company, 2002.

Wilson-Smith, Timothy. *Joan of Arc: Maid, Myth and History*. Gloucester: Sutton Publishing, 2006.

An Invitation

Reader, the book that you hold in your hands was published by Sophia Institute Press. Sophia Institute seeks to nurture the spiritual, moral, and cultural life of souls and to spread the gospel of Christ in conformity with the authentic teachings of the Roman Catholic Church.

Our press fulfills this mission by offering translations, reprints, and new publications that afford readers a rich source of the enduring wisdom of mankind.

We also operate two popular online Catholic resources: CrisisMagazine.com and CatholicExchange.com.

Crisis Magazine provides insightful cultural analysis that arms readers with the arguments necessary for navigating the ideological and theological minefields of the day. *Catholic Exchange* provides world news from a Catholic perspective as well as daily devotionals and articles that will help you grow in holiness and live a life consistent with the teachings of the Church.

In 2013, Sophia Institute launched Sophia Institute for Teachers to renew and rebuild Catholic culture through service to Catholic education. With the goal of nurturing the spiritual, moral, and cultural life of souls, and an abiding respect for the role and work of teachers, we strive to provide materials and programs that are at once enlightening to the mind and ennobling to the heart; faithful and complete, as well as useful and practical.

www.SophiaInstitute.com
www.CatholicExchange.com
www.CrisisMagazine.com
www.SophiaInstituteforTeachers.org

Sophia Institute Press® is a registered trademark of Sophia Institute. Sophia Institute is a tax-exempt institution as defined by the Internal Revenue Code, Section 501(c)(3). Tax I.D. 22-2548708.